The Science of Engineering Attraction & Love: Flirt, Date, and Mate Using Human Psychology

By Patrick King
Social Interaction Specialist and
Conversation Coach
www.PatrickKingConsulting.com

Table of Contents

Introduction

Michael is a long-time client, and when I think back to where we started, it's startling.

When we first met, he characterized himself as an introvert, although I quickly learned that his self-assessment was mostly a cover for his lack of social confidence and lack of confidence in general.

He was 29 years old, had never had a girlfriend, and had never even kissed a girl. I knew something deeper than just being an introvert was holding him back. Long before we met, he had made assumptions about how to treat women, and no one had ever corrected him or showed him why those assumptions were wrong.

With my prompting, he began to use online dating sites and dating apps. He was able to get some matches, and one of our first coaching sessions was about how to keep a conversation going with a woman.

Michael wasn't boring or off-putting in conversation; he just needed to learn how to structure a conversation to be more interesting. He showed me a text conversation between him and a female friend whom he was interested in—that's when a pattern became obvious.

If his goal was to make his female friend like him in the way he wanted her to, he was accomplishing absolutely the opposite.

1. He was sending her three texts for every one she sent, and although her replies were one sentence at most, his were voluminous. If his texts had been green

and hers blue, the screen would have looked like the fairway on a golf course.

2. He was making it painfully clear that he was constantly clearing his entire schedule for her and that spending even a minute of time with her was his first, second, and third priority. He said as much explicitly and made sure to always inquire about her availability weeks in advance.

3. He was sending the text equivalent of chain email messages such as "How's your Monday going?" and "Happy hump day!" just to be able to start conversations that had died the previous day.

Michael's initial question to me was about why she seemed to be pulling away even though they had so much fun when they hung out. I had my own ideas about how those hangouts actually went and why she was getting as cold as a glacier toward him.

The answer is likely plain as day to you as well: too much, too eager, too available, all too soon.

When you smother someone, you burglarize their independence and make it seem as if you have nothing better to do with your time. You are perceived as someone with low social value and even less sexual attraction. There's no mystery or compelling reason for others to be interested in you because you've already presented them with everything they could want from you.

I told him as much, and my explanation hinged on understanding people's psychology and what makes them want something. Ultimately, it all boils down to the unconscious triggers that make people act one way versus another. It was logical and instinctual, but there was no hard evidence I could generally use to explain it.

You generally know the logic, but it can be difficult to articulate because your argument can also be boiled down to "Well, this is my opinion from my experiences." I had plenty of anecdotal knowledge from my own experiences and even those of other clients, but I thought there must be other things I could draw on to support my advice and opinion.

This got me thinking—I know that I have a pretty good chance of being correct when I make reads like that, but was there a way I could bolster and improve my understanding of what makes people act unconsciously? Even better, could I find peer-reviewed studies of the unconscious markers that create effective flirting, lead to sex, and emulate love?

This book takes what I have learned about human psychology and combines it with hard evidence to give you a real path toward engineering attraction and feelings of love. It takes actions you perform sometimes but don't know why and gives you a nifty guideline to follow to actually create the effect you intended to subconsciously.

Everyone likes to parade their opinion as gospel, but that's because they form their opinions based on a sample size of one— themselves. Here, let's use the data from thousands and let you date better based on facts and evidence, which actually provides an objective solution to your dating troubles.

The solution for Michael's texting woes was simpler than most because it played mostly on one psychological factor—*availability*.

Therefore, my prescription for him was to avoid always initiating the conversation, to match the intervals of her replies, to actively spend time with other women, and to be less available when making plans with her.

Most situations are much more complex, but when you can make something as unpredictable as emotion a little bit more predictable, it gives you a massive advantage in generating the type of attraction you've always wanted. Hopefully you are able to use this book as part textbook and part instruction for that very purpose.

Chapter 1. Animal Attraction

Looking at attraction through the lens of biology is actually the purest way to see it.

All the trappings of modern-day society— Ferraris, tiny bikinis, sprawling mansions, pick-up lines—work toward the exact same purpose. They create attraction in an instinctual and almost animalistic way that we can't really rationalize to ourselves. They excite and release hormones, and then *something* happens. It's happened for thousands of years, and only recently have we as a species been able to study ourselves adequately.

Often, we don't fully understand our own actions, but they can usually be boiled down to one of the factors presented in this chapter. This is because it's been hard-coded in our genes to be attracted to aspects and traits that indicate that someone will be a *good* partner in biological terms.

We can see this in our conscious actions: in the beginning phases of dating someone new, you do this to the 10th degree. You pay for everything, you put your best face and outfit on, you act courteously, and you generally try to make your best impression. You make sure to use copious amounts of deodorant and perfume and showcase your talents and skills. We present all our positives while subtly obscuring our negative traits and shortcomings. This influences everything from haircuts to wearing high-heeled shoes.

How do we see these effects in our subconscious actions? Well, some of the aforementioned *conscious* actions are *subconscious* to some! Just because something seems like a no-brainer in terms of attracting a mate doesn't mean it's a no-brainer to everyone. Why do men suddenly suck in their guts and puff out their chest when a beautiful woman enters the room, and why do women flip their hair and also puff out their chests when a handsome man walks in? If someone doesn't realize they are doing that by instinct, imagine how many of our actions or criteria for mates we are simply using by unexamined reflex?

The point is, our ways of generating attraction are mostly subconscious and mostly biological and evolutionary by nature. Even the way you talk to the opposite sex and attempt to flirt has roots and Is not a product of random chance. It explains why you tend to be attracted to certain types of people and even why certain types repulse you.

At the most base level, this is best summed up with the *sociobiological theory of attraction*, which puts everything through the perspective of propagating our offspring. In other words, what determines attractiveness in each gender is what enhances the likelihood of children and genetic offspring.

Men will seek young, attractive women—women who can physically bear children and aren't sexually involved with others so as to reduce the chance of raising another male's children. Women will seek men not necessarily based on physical strength, but rather on power and dominance within a society. They are seeking to provide safety and security for their children, and that can be found in many forms. You can already see how this theory plays out in our modern era.

You can see the common stereotypes of men being more physically shallow, while women are more financially shallow. Could it actually be true, for non-nefarious, subconscious biological reasons? Who knows.

Four Sequential Steps to Attraction

To delve more deeply into the instinctual markers of attraction, researcher Eric Waisman put forth a proposal of four specific components of attraction that shed some light on the sociobiological theory of attraction.

They are not hard rules, but rather general features people tend to look for in a partner, which happen to highly relate to biological drives. In the past, they represented a mate that was going to help you bear your children and protect them effectively. Articulating our subconscious desires is helpful in understanding why we are drawn to some people and even how we can improve our own attractiveness to the opposite (or same) sex.

Waisman's four types of attraction are:
1. Health
2. Status
3. Emotion
4. Logic

Interestingly, the order of those is also the chronological flow that must be followed for attraction to occur. This means each step is necessary for the next level of attraction to occur and to ultimately lead you into a relationship. When you've hit the fourth attraction factor, logic, it means you are compatible in all the preceding ways, and after the honeymoon dust settles, you will still be able to stand being around each other.

In a nutshell, here's how Waisman's attraction flow works:

You must first be physically healthy for anyone to take notice →
Next, you must be capable of providing what is biologically expected of your gender →
Next, you must be emotionally attractive and have romantic chemistry to feel lasting attachment →
Finally, a relationship can form if you share similar values, goals, and worldviews.

Once again, you don't have to look far to see the accuracy of these attraction types. They mirror the actual dating process almost exactly. If you spot someone at a bar or club, well, you wouldn't spot them if you didn't think they were physically attractive. Once you began talking to them, you'd feel more attracted to them if they had more power and status versus a career as a burger flipper.

After you'd gone out with them a couple of times, their dimples and physical attractiveness wouldn't be enough to sustain a relationship; you'd need to feel emotional bonding to them. But even all those prerequisites wouldn't be enough unless you had similar values and conceptions of how you wanted to live; if someone wanted to move to Alaska to hunt whales and your favorite movie was *Free Willy*, it might not work out.

Let's take a deeper dive into each part of the process. Step one is *health*.

When you meet someone, you first notice their physical appearance and attractiveness. At the very least, you notice if you find them physically unattractive or repulsive. More important, you notice if you are, or could be, sexually attracted to them. If you can't see them in that light, at least potentially, then the opportunity for attraction stops right there. The next levels don't even come into play because there would seemingly be no end goal.

It's why we groom ourselves, dress nicely, and go to the gym. We want to appear sexually viable, and we understand that shallow first impressions do indeed matter.

Of course, this is the origin of the so-called *friend zone*. Someone may check the boxes on the other types of attraction, but they aren't a sexually viable person, so there's really no amount of emotional support that can overcome that and they are generally doomed to friend status in perpetuity.

We are drawn to people we find physically attractive—not a radical idea. If you'd like to have sex with them or can imagine having sex with them, you've passed the first level of attraction.

It sounds shallow, and it might be, but it's how real-world attraction functions. It's only in romantic comedies that the hero ends up with the dumpy-looking best friend who has their best interests at heart! You can either play the game to win or decide to opt out and continually lose.

Most things we do to attract others target this attraction point because it's what people's first impression. Therefore, hitting the gym, making over your wardrobe, getting regular haircuts, trimming your nails, shaving occasionally, applying make-up, wearing high-heeled shoes—all help, no matter how much you want to believe otherwise.

This is a clear, easy-to-read signpost for what we can work on. First impressions are made in a split second, so focusing your efforts on everything visible during that initial impression should be your first priority in becoming more attractive. If you understood that it was a true gatekeeper for you, how would you improve or change your appearance?

How viable of a mate would you appear to be

if someone were basing their attraction to you on only this factor?

Step two: is their status great enough for you?

This is commonly known as the resume phase—how do they look on paper? Being brutally frank, this is the phase that causes us to ask, "Are they beneath me? Will they be worth my time? Do they check the boxes that I am looking for?"

After you're physically attracted to someone, the next step is to think about how eligible that person is and whether they will be able to provide for you in the way that you expect their gender to. No one wants their partner to be dead weight or a leech, and most people would like their partner to have the means to do the kinds of things they want to do. This isn't just about money, but money *is* certainly a large part of the equation. Status hearkens back to the sociobiological theory of women wanting support and safety and men seeking overall fertility.

The stereotypical gold digger would skip right to this attraction point, as would the stereotypical man looking for a trophy wife. The first two attraction points are the more superficial filters, and many a relationship has sustained itself on these for short periods of time. However, they may or may not be the most fulfilling or deep relationships.

Even though it's clearly important because none of us want to live in a shoebox, we lie to ourselves and refuse to give importance to this because we believe it instantly brands us as shallow and materialistic. But does it?

Evolutionarily speaking, no. Status began with wanting the leader of the pack, village, or tribe to ensure you would be protected and safe. You don't even have to come up with an analogy for that description to fit into the modern day.

Traditional gender roles play strong here. A man with status has power, money, and prestige. A woman with status has beauty, fertility, and nurturing instincts. It's a large part of the emotional bond that we like to deny, but evidence is available any time you venture into public. If there is a mismatch in physical attractiveness, often it's easy to see exactly why someone is with someone else.

The attraction of status is an evolutionary safeguard to survival.

The third factor essentially asks the following question: wait, do I actually *like* this person?

Do you have interpersonal chemistry, emotional attraction, and feelings of being drawn to them? Do you miss them when they aren't present? Do you share their sense of humor or at least appreciate their humor?

This is where *romantic love* finally comes into play—well, actually, scratch that. This is just where *getting along* comes into play. It might be surprising to see the notion of romantic love being demoted so far, but it's hard to deny that other factors take precedent, at least chronologically, before you can actually consider romantic love.

Look at the previous factors of health and status as the windows and windshield of a car. You can't drive the car without those, so you need to fulfill the basic needs first before you can hit the highway, so to speak. It's something we'd all like to imagine is our top priority when we're looking at a mate, but that's a lie that evolution likes to obscure with other types of attraction.

Romeo and Juliet certainly had emotional attraction, but look what happened to them. You can probably think of other examples where a couple seemed destined for each other but other factors tore them apart.

This naturally begs the question, if we're not marrying for love, what are we marrying for? It's time to expand the notion of love, because it comprises many things that romantic comedy movies like to ignore.

Many of us allow feelings of romantic love and infatuation to take charge, but contrary to love songs, love is *not* all you need. There still remains the question of how truly compatible you are—not in personality, but in terms of worldview and values.

That's what the fourth stage is about: logic. You like (and maybe even love) each other, you get along well, you're physically attracted to each other, and you have a healthy financial prognosis.

But those are all still short-term concerns. What about thinking long-term? Surely those aren't enough to sustain a marriage, are they?

It makes you ask questions such as:

- Can this relationship go the distance?
- Do we have the same life goals?
- Do we both want children?
- Do we share similar values?
- Will we be happy in five years?
- And perhaps most important, can I live with the other person's flaws or are they deal-breakers?

The logic phase questions whether it makes sense from a *rational perspective* to have a relationship with the other person.

The most common example of a relationship fizzling out because of logic is a vacation fling. Perhaps you've connected with another person, and everything seems incredibly in sync... but you've only spent 48 hours together and you live on opposite sides of the world. That's where logic steps in and sorts things out.

As you can see, the first two factors are more superficial and short-sighted, while the latter two factors are more introspective and indicative of a relationship's actual success.

Now visualize how many couples you know who have created relationships that depend solely on the first two (or three) attraction factors and have completely ignored the latter factors. It's no surprise that some couples fight like cats and dogs and are doomed to failure—they didn't align the types of attraction that matter long-term.

Visualize a couple where the male wants children but the female does not. What does that mean for the long-term potential of that relationship, no matter how physically attracted they are to each other?

Logical attraction focuses primarily on our morals, values, and what is important to us in the world.

For example, do you want to get married? Do you want to have children after you get married? Do you have the same goals as far as career advancement and financial security are concerned? Do you want to live in Chicago forever or move around Asia for years at a time? Do you share the same religion?

Logic deals with deal-breakers.

We look at the people we can potentially date and sort them into yes and no piles based on their values. It's as simple as imagining whether a risk-averse corporate lawyer could ever truly be happy with a country-hopping nomadic soap salesman. Could they be attracted to each other?

This logical analysis is very linear. You look at core similarities and you project from there. The more you can imagine the possibility of a relationship, the more attractive the other person becomes.

The four attractions clearly spell out the steps you need to take to become attractive, and they prompt you to anticipate major issues that can become problems so that you can save your valuable time. Chances are, if you are skipping a step, you aren't an exception to the rule. You just haven't seen where the dust will settle.

Which among these four steps do you lack, and which are strengths you can capitalize on? Where in the process do you continually get stuck? These are the questions you can start to answer for yourself with your newfound knowledge.

Takeaways:

- The classic sociobiological theory of attraction states that we are nothing but animals when it comes to attraction. Worse yet, most of what we are attracted to is subconscious and not fully understood.
- Waisman's four steps are an elaboration on the classic sociobiological theory of attraction. They inform us as to exactly what we are looking for in a way that fuses sociobiological theory with modern dating.
- The four attractions are physical, status, emotion, and logic. It is a sequence you must pass through for a deep and fulfilling relationship, although we know many that only satisfied two or three factors in their own relationships.
- The best way to use these four factors is to understand what phase you are in when you are evaluating someone and to understand where you may fall short.

Chapter 2. Don't Say a Word

As you may or may not be aware, studies pegged the importance of nonverbal body language: between 55% and 93% of the entire message we communicate to others is nonverbal and unrelated to the words coming out of your mouth. The amounts may differ from study to study and context to context, but the overall message is the same. It's not what you say; it's *how* you say it and how you look.

Naturally, this is going to transfer seamlessly to flirting and attraction, perhaps even more so because flirting involves a heavy number of cues and operates within gray areas. If this is important in everyday situations like school and work, imagine how important it is in engineering attraction and love.

The overall lesson of this chapter is to arm you with knowledge about what types of nonverbal body language are most attractive to the opposite sex, what to look for in evaluating the interest level of other people, and how to use this knowledge to make yourself attractive before you even open your mouth.

Various studies by Helen Fisher, Allen Pease, and Barbara Pease were able to articulate two main traits of body language that are both indicative of interest and attractive to others on an instinctive level and from an evolutionary standpoint.

Body Language

Surprisingly, the studies showed that the first aspect of attractive and effective body language is *availability*.

This means that you appear to be open, welcoming, friendly, and willing to engage.

Smiles, uncrossed legs, eye contact, and a torso that is pointed fully toward the other person indicate availability. Think about it; how does someone who uses all of those body language gestures simultaneously appear to you? You would probably be less nervous to speak with them than someone with crossed arms and a mean look on their face. You'd feel that you would be welcomed instead of pushed away. You might feel like they are friendly and that you have a chance, which is always the first step to engaging.

Availability means there is, in theory, a decreased chance of rejection, and that is attractive because it feels as if it is within our grasp. If you have a chance, you're automatically more interested because it's more likely to be a better use of your time. Here, love and attraction shows itself as opportunistic.

How this comes across in body language is relatively simple—just be aware of closed and unavailable body language to start with. Start by eliminating the negative, and think about how open, vulnerable, and welcoming you make your body when you are approaching a puppy. It's a useful mental image for how to appear more available and overall attractive.

The second aspect of attractive and effective body language is how *fertile* you appear. *Fertile* is a term that refers to how powerful and effective a mate someone would be—as you can imagine, there are very different standards for men and women.

This goes back to understanding what we look for in each gender and the sociobiological theory of attraction from the previous chapter. Think back to traditional gender roles and the adjectives we use to describe each of them. What makes a man sexually attractive versus what makes a woman sexually attractive on a purely biological level? Now, how can you reflect those through your body language?

The body language of a biologically attractive man is dominant and powerful.

Attractive males embody the triangle-shaped

body—broad shoulders that taper down to a thinner waist. They take up space with their shoulders and arms and try to emphasize their muscle mass with their posture. The bigger they can appear, the better (think of a peacock spreading its tail feathers). The more they can separate and distinguish themselves from other males, the better. The more dominant and deep the eye contact, the better.

Male fertility is about the ability to be a dominant mate who can protect his own, something that masculine body language signifies.

Males may also preen like peacocks, groom themselves, and make bodily movements to attract the attention of nearby females. It's all a show to draw attention to their alpha male traits. They compete for attention and mates, and everything is geared toward winning that competition.

Unsure what this looks like? Just imagine how differently a roomful of men would suddenly look if a supermodel walked in. Everyone's spines would straighten, stomachs would be sucked in, chests puffed out, and voices would deepen and get louder. They might each attempt to become the center of attention to show social influence and power. All this behavior might not even be conscious, but instinctually we understand that each gender is biologically programmed to project *fertile* body language.

If any men need guidance on how their body language should ideally be for flirtation and attraction, just think of the cartoon character *Johnny Bravo*, but not so over the top. Everyone has their preferences, but the body language Johnny Bravo exhibits, with his huge upper body and expansive motions, is undeniably masculine and generally more preferred than a male that exhibits none of those things.

The ideal body language for a sexually attractive woman on the other hand, is stunningly different.

In contrast to the triangle-shaped male, the female ideal is the hourglass figure. A woman is seen as more attractive if she appears graceful, soft, and curvy and slender at the same time. Femininity is all soft curves and supple flesh because female fertility is about the ability to give birth to multiple children and remain healthy.

Women want to accentuate the curves of an hourglass-shaped body. Put a woman in a pair of heels and have her walk past a row of attractive men. Notice how her gait changes, how it emphasizes her hips and bust and she suddenly acts like she is walking down a fashion runway.

Other indicators of fertility for females are the lips and hair—health is reflected in how healthy these physical traits are. This means the body language for an attractive female is to emphasize those physical traits and draw attention to them—hence lip-biting and hair-flipping.

If any woman needs guidance about how

their body language should ideally be for flirtation and attraction, just think about Jessica Rabbit from the movie *Who Framed Roger Rabbit?* and how she saunters across a room. There's a reason so many men see her as the one cartoon they would sleep with without question.

This approach isn't about looking for specific signs—it's about thinking along the lines of availability and fertility. If you're still having trouble imagining how this plays out for the different genders, just imagine how 10 women would pose for a picture versus how 10 men would. They instinctively pop their hips and shoulders and attempt to create the illusion of curves and fertility to create a favorable hip-to-waist-to-breast ratio. You'll have a real-life illustration of how it plays out, and you'll be able to see exactly why the poses end up so differently. You can also consider how ancient Greek statues portray the different genders in a stark contrast of hard angles versus soft curves.

The vast majority of the messages we send to

other people and to the world are nonverbal. Knowing the biological and evolutionary basis for what's attractive will help you see these signs and fulfill them yourself.

It's easy to overlook these aspects as "common sense" or as something you are already doing, but in reality, are you?

That's why it's so important to bring light to what have been proven to be objectively (as much as there can be in the field of attraction) attractive body language. Make sure you are ticking off the biologically proven triggers first, because it is unlikely you are acting in such an arousing way as to override people's evolutionary sensibilities.

Eye Contact

Of course, eye contact is the other main component of how we perceive attraction and even rate it. As a society, we view eye contact as imperative to attracting a mate.

The sheer number of eye-related idioms and

sayings in English confirms that people truly believe eyes are the key to someone's mind and heart.

Shifty eyes, bedroom eyes, kind eyes, knowing eyes, dead eyes, the Evil Eye.

Are they right? Actually, it doesn't really matter.

The belief in the transparency of eye contact is so widespread that your eye contact must be good or you will be labeled with a host of negative adjectives. The same belief applies to body language. Do certain types of body language really reveal that you are inherently a good or bad person? Not always, but people's beliefs make it so that you need to make sure that your external signals create attraction and not distrust.

So as a general matter, eye contact is a prerequisite to appearing trustworthy, loyal, and confident. In the context of attraction however, it is even more important because it creates a sense of sexual tension that people thrive on. Sexual tension is difficult to define, but with eye contact, it's generating a feeling of slight discomfort and excitement at processing the forwardness of extended eye contact. Tension is one of the huge drivers of human attraction and sexuality, and resolving that tension is often a motivator for all things dating.

It's the kind of tension that says, "*I know you know... but do you know that I know that you know?*" or *"I want you and my eyes are doing the work instead of my hands."*

Fortunately for you, most people are flat-out *bad* at eye contact. If you are even halfway decent at eye contact, you have a huge leg up on most people in creating sexual tension with the opposite sex or even just appearing trustworthy in a job interview. Just think about the people in your office that have a tough time meeting your gaze, to the point of appearing like they are avoiding you.

If you can handle the tension and discomfort that comes with extended eye contact, attraction will be far easier to generate. Remember, you are trying to create tension, so if you are comfortable with it, you have a higher tolerance to create more of it with others.

How can you go about generating the kind of tension that makes someone's heart beat out of their chest? Thanks to Kellerman et al. in 1989 ("Looking and Loving: The Effects of Mutual Gaze on Feelings of Romantic Love"), we have a straightforward guideline.

Effective eye contact is in the *delivery*. Controlling the quantity of eye contact you give is important, but if you have too much, you turn the corner from flirtatious to looking like you are imagining skinning them alive. More eye contact is not necessarily better, so be intentional with the delivery of your eye contact.

This is best demonstrated with the concept of "sticky eyes." The name comes from the fact that you should act as if your eyes are attached the other person's eyes with a sticky, oozing glue.

What happens with sticky, oozing glues? They don't keep things rigidly stuck, they simply slow the rate of movement.

When you look away from their eyes and break eye contact, your eyes should linger on theirs, even after you start turning your head. Let the strand of glue keep your eyes on theirs long after it would normally end, as if you can't look away from them. Give them the impression that you are reluctant to look away at all, that you can't take your eyes off of them even though you need to engage with someone else.

You're putting the spotlight on them with your eyes. Then every time you make sustained eye contact (make sure it's more of a gaze versus a stare—a television news anchor *stares*, while you *gaze* at puppies playing in the park) imagine that the glue makes them feel like the apple of your eye.

That means that your eye contact motions are

slow and intentional, and there are no quick movements. Even your blinks are deliberate and slow. You don't flick your eyes to the side as you usually would, and you don't scan the room or their face quickly as you would with other people. You don't react to small ancillary things happening around you and let them interrupt your gaze.

It's as if nothing can drag you away from their eyes. Sticky eyes are the epitome of bedroom eyes: seductive, intense, inquisitive, and suggestive.

Sticky eyes create anticipation because you are telling the other person something with your eyes. You will make them feel turned on and slightly self-conscious, but not in a negative way—self-conscious in that you are appreciating them and they are recognizing it. There's a high likelihood of a blush.

Prolonged eye contact can be very intense for some, and you can scare people off if you don't calibrate the amount you use to what they seem comfortable with. It's a low-grade violation of personal space, so you have to be careful about how you wield it.

Not everyone will be comfortable with it, and not everyone will know how to receive sticky eyes. It's just too much tension for some and will make them retreat—like how we are compelled to change the channel if a movie scene comes on where the character is so cringe-inducing that we actually feel physical discomfort.

Instead of pairing face-to-face interaction with sticky eyes, try standing at the person's side when you make sustained eye contact. Let them feel that their personal space is still completely intact, and they will be more comfortable with your sticky eyes and feel less of a need to defend themselves and disengage. This has the added bonus of allowing you to get closer physically— shoulder to shoulder—than you would if you were face to face. Being face to face with someone before they're ready can feel uncomfortable at best and threatening or distressing at worst.

This point about approaching from the side sheds light on a couple of things.

First, everyone has their own struggles, and you might actually be in the position of power when it comes to eye contact. Keep an eye out for this and make sure that you aren't going to intimidate them in any way.

Second, there truly is such a thing as too much eye contact. Eye contact inherently is direct and inquisitive, and if you happen on someone who isn't comfortable with either of those things, they will recoil. You need to adjust to the person if your goal is to actually attract them.

Each of us has a certain amount of tolerance for personal space invasion. For some, you could have your hands in their pockets and they wouldn't care, but for others, simple eye contact face to face can feel like too much. You have to adapt and calibrate to everyone's tolerance level, and you can compensate for strong eye contact by giving them additional physical space.

For further illustration, let's think about why Catholic confessionals and couches in psychiatrist's offices are arranged to reduce the amount of eye contact between the involved parties. Or why it's hard to look at someone in the eye when you are making an emotional or intimate observation. Eye contact is a huge aspect of personal space, and if you feel that you are baring yourself in other ways, reducing the amount of eye contact can help compensate.

Tension is good; too much tension makes you seem like a serial killer. You should apply the knowledge in this chapter thus far in two ways: to understand how to make yourself more attractive and to read people better to understand if they are attracted to you.

The next level of creating attraction without saying a word is through touching, of course.

Strategic Touching

Is it a surprise that touch has a huge scientific basis for attraction? It's what causes our knees to wobble and butterflies to flutter around in our stomachs.

The lightest and subtlest touch, done correctly, can be the difference between seeing someone as a sexual object versus forever seeing them as only a friend. It can be a brush on the shoulder, a hand on the knee, and even a lingering handshake.

In the best (or worst) scenario, a touch can even make you light-headed and faint— maybe that's the origin of the phrase *starry-eyed love*?

With how important touching is to courtship and attraction, it makes sense that there is an optimal way to touch others to enhance the attraction they feel for you. In fact, there are optimal ways, combinations, and types of touching that you should use to seduce others, male or female.

Your first step is to take a deep breath and

break the touch barrier in general. Here's why: normally, acquaintances only touch in a particular, careful, unambiguous, mutually understood way. They shake hands or hug when they greet, or they might give a slap on the shoulder in acknowledgment of a joke or a job well done. These are all common and accepted ways of touching among people who know each other well and are friends or colleagues. There's only a certain threshold the touching will reach in a platonic manner.

Touching someone beyond that threshold instantly raises an eyebrow internally and instantly puts you into a different light. Touch alone can plant the seed of courtship. Attraction only works if you are seen as a sexual being, and sexual beings touch. Touching beyond that threshold sends an unambiguous message that there is attraction and interest. It's as close as you can get to saying that you are interested without using actual words. You wouldn't have to tell someone, "I like you and want to date you," if you always gave them extended hugs and put your hand on their knee during a movie.

So when someone senses that, it's natural that they will begin to consider the toucher in that light as well. Touching also implies boldness, sexuality, and not being passive or shy—all of which are typically attractive in the opposite sex.

A big roadblock many people have with dating is falling into the friend zone—and the absence of touching is the very thing that leads them there. All other signs of interest or attraction are much more ambiguous and leave room for interpretation—touching sends just one message: I find you sexually attractive.

Now how can we touch strategically and effectively?

In a 2007 study by Nicolas Gueguen ("Courtship Compliance: The Effect of Touch on Women's Behavior"), scientists identified three distinct categories of touch, and their different uses and consequences. They also found the exact combination to use to flirt and get your message across more effectively.

The three types of touching are:

1. Friendly touching
2. Plausible deniability touching
3. Nuclear touching

Let's discuss each of these in more detail.

The first category, *friendly touching*, is the type of touch I spoke about earlier, the kind you'd engage in with coworkers and friends. Actually, it's the type of touch you might even share with a stranger and give no second thought to because it's so casual and sometimes unavoidable.

Examples of friendly touching are handshakes, taps on the shoulder, a hand on the upper arm, high fives, and even bumping into someone else.

Friendly touching is intentional, yet harmless. It doesn't advance attraction and in fact might be used to set a platonic tone. There is no subtext, and this kind of touching is exactly what it appears to be. It is not the kind of touching that sends a deeper message.

If you stick to this category of touch, it won't register at all that any flirting is occurring because it is so incidental and accepted. You could even do this with a stranger or someone you just met—although it's normally reserved for people you know (but not people you have a sexual or romantic interest in). There are no second thoughts given when you use friendly touch, and thus no attraction is created.

Obviously, this is the type of touch that is least related to attraction and flirting, but many people still attempt to send messages through it because they don't feel bold enough for other types of touch.

For example, thinking "I touched his back for a split second longer as I was trying to get by him, so he definitely has to know what I'm thinking" is fairly common thinking—even though it was objectively the kind of touch you might use on a coworker to move past them in the hallway of your office.

Part of the problem with touching is it's mostly relative, which means that people have different standards for what constitutes "a lot" and "only a little" touching. This is why there are so many mixed and failed messages, even though these three distinct categories of touching exist. Learning to distinguish between the three types of touch will help you understand the exact type of message you are sending to others.

The second category of touch is called *plausible deniability touching*.

First things first—plausible deniability is when you create a situation where you could have a plausible claim that the touch was either unintentional or that it had no particular motive. So, yes, you've touched someone, but there is doubt about why you did so or whether you had any specific intention. The touch is over the threshold of a simple friendly touch, but you aren't sure if it was by accident or intentional—and the key is to get someone thinking about what you meant. Once you have people wondering, you're *in*.

People won't know what to make of you because your touching appears to be above the level of friendly touching—it definitely borders on flirtatious and deliberate, but the touching is contextual and incidental to some degree, so people are left wondering what you actually intended.

For example, buckling someone else's seat belt for them. This can be done in a relatively clinical manner, though your hands will definitely enter private zones on the other person's body. The plausible deniability here is just that you are in a hurry or you wanted to help someone buckle their seat belt. It raises eyebrows but is also acceptable in the context. Another example is when you fix someone's hair or find any flimsy excuse to be in a person's face or personal space. Maybe you're there to make a move, or maybe you're there for a perfectly legitimate reason and you shouldn't be presumptuous!

You are in a gray area when you touch people this way, and that's effective because you can essentially touch a lot but not directly show your hand, so to speak. This is extremely effective for flirting and playing the game because you are sending an effective mixed message. On one hand, you are touching a lot and nearly violating their normal boundaries, but on the other hand, perhaps you just want to help them buckle their seat belt.

The important part is that they'll be thinking about you and your touch—you'll be on their mind. The first step to having sex with someone is to have them envision it, and that's exactly what this type of touch does. It makes a suggestion, but it also raises a question and makes your intentions mysterious enough to keep them wondering.

Flirting works best when there is a degree of uncertainty in the equation and you don't know exactly what the other person is thinking. It's like a game of cat and mouse, but each person thinks they are the cat. It's easy to see why plausible deniability touching can work wonders—the uncertainty is thrilling, just like a sports match would be far less interesting if you already knew the outcome.

Here are some additional opportunities for plausible deniability touching:
- Giving someone a brief shoulder massage
- Comparing the size of your hands (or other body part) with theirs by placing that body part next to theirs—as in placing your palms together
- Asking to examine something close to them, such as a piece of their clothing
- Holding someone's hip or waist to pull them in one direction
- Demonstrating a physical act (like a salsa dance move) on them
- Using your body to bump someone out of the way of something while you are walking together

Let your imagination run wild on this. Just remember that you need a plausible alternative explanation for being in someone's space, and your goal here is to be direct but also sow uncertainty.

The third category of touching as it pertains to flirting and attraction is dubbed *nuclear touching*.

This is where the rubber hits the road—there is no ambiguity here about your intentions and level of attraction. You meant to touch the person that way, and you meant something very deliberate by it.

Visualize a scenario where you know a kiss is imminent. What kind of slow, seductive touching would you use in the moments building up to that kiss? This is where you're making a statement and putting yourself out there for a potential rejection, which is something the other two types of touches explicitly avoid.

There are three main measures of nuclear-level touching. First, *where* are you touching? Nuclear touching occurs in zones that other types don't venture near. It's difficult to mistake your intent when you touch someone directly on their lips, grab their buttocks firmly, or pull someone between your legs. There can be no plausible deniability for any of those actions. Other areas that cause a nuclear reaction besides the obvious erogenous areas are the neck, face, and belly.

Second, is the touch by itself, or is it *combined* with other signs of attraction and flirting like sustained eye contact and a lowered tone of voice? Touch by itself is one thing, but it is amplified when done simultaneously with other signs of deep attraction and flirting.

Third, how *deliberate* do you appear? For example, if you slid your hand onto someone's buttocks and they looked at you shocked, would you just smile and not move your hand, or would you immediately back off and apologize for being too forward? These two different responses from you demonstrate markedly different levels of intent and attraction.

Nuclear touching can be difficult to define,

but you just know it when you see or feel it. You'll feel a rush of blood to your cheeks— and maybe elsewhere.

Now that you understand the three different categories of touching, is it possible to diagnose your flirting issues by the types of touch you've neglected or used ineffectively?

Perhaps you only use friendly touching and don't send the message you intend to. You'll think you are subtly sending a message, but in reality, you are just treating someone like a new friend. Or maybe you use nuclear touching too much and it scares people off or makes you seem predatory and overly aggressive.

The study went on to suggest that the most effective type of touching is actually a combination of plausible deniability and nuclear touching, with friendly touching not making much of an impact at all.

This shouldn't be surprising if we consider that flirting thrives in uncertainty and creates a push (they like me) and pull (they don't like me), and this combination creates the very same effect. The power is in the combination, because each type, used by itself, doesn't convey the message you intend.

For example, friendly touching by itself just makes you appear to be the friendly type at work or in social situations.

If you overuse plausible deniability and never let it slide into nuclear touching—so that there is no question of your intent— eventually the other person will lose interest. They will assume you are either clumsy or without couth; they won't assume you have an interest in them. You will have disguised yourself too well!

If you use nuclear touch too much, it can be too direct and aggressive and will not create mystery for the other person to wonder about. Or you'll just get slapped. If you make your intentions too direct and don't give them a chance to process things for themselves, their fight-or-flight mode will be activated.

They might just panic and retreat.

If there is a single lesson to be taken from this chapter, it's that you have to make yourself a sexual object. This is the biggest failing of the so-called friend-zoned men and women—they hope to show their potential as a mate through everything but sex. But we are, at our root, just hairless primates that want sex—so make yourself sexually viable with touch, body language, and eye contact.

Takeaways:

- Many animals don't have verbal languages. This means they must communicate their attraction, often forcefully, through their movements and actions. The human equivalent is how we communicate nonverbally with our body language, eye contact, and touching.
- There are different types of attractive body language for each gender. They do, however, depend on the factors of availability and fertility. Simply put, the more available you appear, the more

attractive you will be, and the more fertile (this varies by gender) you appear, the more attractive you will be.

- We all know eye contact is import, but it goes beyond simple trustworthiness and confidence. If you are able to use the "sticky eyes" technique, you will begin to create the discomfort and excitement of sexual tension.
- There have been found to be three types of touching in the context of flirting and attraction: friendly, plausible deniability, and nuclear. The most ideal mix is plausible deniability touching mixed with nuclear touching because of the message it sends and how it balances itself out. Friendly touching doesn't really factor into it, even though that's what we are most accustomed to.

Chapter 3. The "Chase"

Dating advice is one of the most prevalent topics in the world.

No matter where you go and no matter the culture you enter, there will always be magazines and books about how to have more success in dating. Why is that?

There are the obvious reasons: that sex, mating, marriage, and everything that follows is a huge part of what we want out of life. They are some of our primary motivators and consume much of our mental bandwidth every day. They represent many of our hopes, dreams, and aspirations and are the cause of many of our greatest triumphs and failures. Whether we realize it or not, we are always priming ourselves for attraction and the possibility of mating in some way or another.

But the other underrated reason dating advice is so prevalent is because it is the epitome of *shades of gray*. There are an almost infinite number of interpretations for every single action because everyone brings their own bias and anecdotal experience to every situation. There can be endless debate, and everyone seems to have an opinion about what to do in certain circumstances. After all, some people like dogs and some like cats. There can surely be a variance in the interpretation of what happens in dating.

The fact is, few people are *subjectively wrong* in their opinions, which further stokes the flames of discussion and debate.

For example, strong eye contact is highly preferred and seen as confident in Western cultures but is threatening and directly confrontational in some Eastern cultures. But it spans beyond obvious cultural differences as well. I might think that my simple act of putting my hand on a woman's back is casual, but she might interpret it as incredibly forward and borderline "creepy" because she was raised in a household where her parents showed no affection for each other.

The underlying point is that you can never be certain that your message will be received as you intended—or received at all. This is especially true in the process of flirting and *chasing*, where you don't want to come on too strong or be weakly and be forgettable.

The Chase

What is *the chase*? There are countless definitions of it.

1. Implanting the idea of your romantic interest in someone so they end up pursuing you
2. How to attract someone covertly and indirectly

3. Conveying romantic interest in a slick and sly way
4. A mind game between two interested parties designed to make the other act first and show their cards
5. How to utilize hot and cold, push and pull behavior to entrance someone romantically
6. How to calibrate the right amount of romantic interest in someone to ignite their attraction to you

Hopefully, one or all of those definitions resonates with you—they all describe mostly the same situation or feeling that we try to create.

Here's what it boils down to: you want to create attraction with others, but you can't show *too much* interest, otherwise you appear too available and low-value. But you can't show *too little* interest, because then people might not even notice your overtures. Basically, you want to strike the right balance of attention and availability for people to see you in the most attractive light.

Even for the people who say that they hate the chase and playing games, they have to admit that they instinctively do things differently when they want someone's attention or affections.

Something odd happens in our minds when someone is too available, too interested, and too eager—and we don't want to be that person! The opposite happens in our minds when someone is unavailable, aloof, and ambiguously interested. We instantly begin to wonder what we're missing and what could be at stake if they suddenly lost interest. We feel like we need to chase them a bit to get back on their radar.

Just imagine how you felt when you knew that someone was *very* interested in you. You might actually be slightly repulsed and turned off. Now imagine that same person showed only occasional signs of interest in such a way that you were never truly sure how they felt about you. How do these situations color your perception of their value? The former makes you question their worth if they are so easy to attain and available. The latter makes you question yourself and your own feelings.

Why do we want what we can't have or aren't certain to attain? Why do we chase or subconsciously try to compel others to chase us? Uncertainty and novelty drive us, while predictability causes complacency and disinterest. The psychological underpinnings of this have been proven over and over in the past century, but first in 1952 by B.F. Skinner in "Intermittent Rewards in Operant Conditioning."

In his landmark study, he provided one group of lab mice with a reward every time they pressed a lever, while another group of mice obtained a reward only randomly after pressing a lever.

The first group received consistent reinforcement, while the second group received intermittent reinforcement, and Skinner discovered that intermittent reinforcement caused the mice to press the lever at a much greater rate than those who received consistent reinforcement.

This tells us that the mice who were rewarded consistently ended up taking it for granted because they knew it would be waiting for them whenever they wanted. They likely got bored because part of the reward for pressing the lever was the anticipation of the reward itself. Whatever the case, they stopped trying as much. The mice who were rewarded inconsistently didn't know when their next reward would come, so they kept pressing the lever to ease their uncertainty.

Coincidentally, this is also the exact psychology behind why gambling and slot machines in particular are so addictive—if you don't know when your reward is coming, you'll be motivated to keep searching for it. Once you finally receive a reward, you'll be immediately looking for your next one because you are so unsatisfied with how long it took.

Intermittent reinforcement is what we try to

accomplish with the chase. We are trying to present ourselves as ambiguously available in order to get someone else to pursue us and become fixated on us. We want to give people just a taste so they are unsatisfied and continue to seek you out for more attention or contact. If you think about your behavior during your pursuit, you'll realize that this creed informed many of your actions.

Observe the chase in action:

- We delay texting back immediately.
- We pretend to be busier than we really are.
- We make our weekends sound more fun than they actually were.
- We avoid people sometimes, even though we want to see them.
- We don't tell people we like them or care about them, even though we do.

We generally attempt to manipulate how available and interested we seem because that's what creates the sense of intermittent reinforcement.

Let's see what constant, consistent reinforcement looks like.

You meet someone with whom you instantly hit it off. You grew up in the same small town, just minutes away from each other, and they share your love of noir fiction and old black-and-white movies.

No games this time, you decide. You've wasted too much of your life strategizing, so you're going to be straightforward and skip the   chase.

So you text them immediately after you get home, and then again in the morning when you wake up. You tell them your entire week is free. You reply to their texts within seconds and tell them about how much your family will like them. You ask whether they like Mexico or Greece for next summer's vacation.

Every time you contact them, they start to look at their phone in disgust because it's too much, too soon, and they've grown tired of the reward you are providing. We prefer a little mystery and intrigue; thus, the more in demand someone is, whether it's work, dating, or friend-related, the more attractive they become.

Of course, instead of spending all this time and effort cultivating an image of a busy person who is in high-demand and unavailable, your time is far better spent actually *being* that high-value person: The type who actually needs to wait hours to text back because they are so occupied. The type who truly only has three free nights in the next two weeks.

Instead of plotting your text timelines and how to reply, become the person that is too busy with their friends, family, hobbies, and passions. It's counterintuitive, but when you're engaged, you become absolutely engaging. Playing the game can feel icky to some, so that's the least positive interpretation of it.

You might not enjoy utilizing the chase, but if

you're going to date, at least play to win—in other words, create a sense of intermittent rewards and mystery.

People say they don't like to play games. If, they say, you can't make someone like you by conventional means, then you didn't deserve them in the first place. Ask people who have been friend-zoned repeatedly how that's worked out for them. Knowing what people are psychologically attracted to is undeniably effective and can often help you cross the line between nothing and a relationship.

Unavailability

Closely related to intermittent reinforcement and the chase is the reality that humans want what we can't have or don't currently possess.

We know this to be true because we have sudden feelings of regret when our attractive friends get into relationships. *What could we be missing out on?*

This was proved in a study by Parker and Burkley. One group of women was presented with a photograph of a handsome man and told he was single, while another group of women was presented with the same photograph and told he was married. Fifty-nine percent of the women were interested in pursuing the single man, but 90% wanted to pursue the married man.

We want what is unavailable to us, especially if we see other indicators of its value and demand. In a vacuum, we may want only what we want, even if no one else wants it. But if someone or something is wanted by many people, then we want it even more. We want to discover for ourselves why they are so desirable and ensure we're not missing an integral piece of information.

When something is easily within our grasp, instead of basking in the triumph of getting it, we think *"Wait, is this even worth having if it's so easy? Could I do better?"* and we don't want it anymore. When that same thing is removed from our realm of possibility or even just made more difficult to attain, we aren't sure if we can attain it, so we feel compelled to keep trying.

This is the essence of playing hard to get. Just remember that you can't play *too* hard to get, otherwise you'll appear uninterested and people will give up. It's *hard* to get, not *impossible* to get.

Studies by Jonason and Li in 2013 identified the types of behaviors that people used when they consciously played hard to get. Do any of these sound familiar?

- Not expressing affection toward their target
- Talking with, flirting with, and even dating other people
- Giving accidental physical contact
- Sarcastic but friendly teasing
- Making others work to spend time with them
- Acting artificially busy
- Flirting and then disappearing; giving attention and then stopping

- Acting disinterested
- Taking a long time to reply to calls or texts

The researchers also asked if these tactics worked in attracting someone they were interested in. They did—every single one of them.

Subjects then rated which respondents (low, medium, high availability) were most attractive to them in given scenarios. High availability was only desirable for short-term relationships. Low availability was just discouraging or preoccupied. The medium availability potential partner was rated the most attractive because they represented someone that was in high demand but was still possible for them to attain.

Shining a flashlight onto the games we subconsciously play may not always be pretty, but it is helpful for you to get who you want. Usually when we turn to games, we have a clear direction of where we want to go. In fact, most of the time, we want to avoid the situation you're about to read about.

"Let's Just Be Friends"

The first time I heard that phrase uttered I was 14 years old. I was crushing on a girl in my Spanish class, Miranda, and I had made an effort to be extra nice to her, help her with her homework, and generally treat her with more attention than I had probably treated any female in my life besides my mother. I began to classify us as close friends.

The whole process began in December, and I remember January turning into February. This was significant because February is the *money* month—it's got Valentine's Day, which was going to be my greatest opportunity to knock her socks off with my grand romantic gestures and make her fall for me.

Remember, I was 14, so let's lower expectations here. I asked my mother to take me to a florist where I bought flowers. I also bought a box of discounted See's Candies because my mother would only allow me to spend $20 on my grand gesture for Miranda.

When Spanish class rolled around on that fateful Valentine's Day, I tapped her on the shoulder and presented her with the flowers and chocolates that had been stuffed into my locker for most of the day.

Her reply? "Let's just be friends." It was a dagger to the heart that took me quite a while to recover from. Is this something you can get around? Is it a real truth that men and women can be truly platonic friends without any romantic complications? Does the chase work here?

The politically correct answer may be to proclaim you can indeed be platonic friends forever. Friendship and sexual attraction are two entirely different measures, and people can separate the two without too much trouble. People can compartmentalize emotions, and people can support and be emotionally intimate with others without romantic or sexual feelings being involved. Friendship is a bond that can transcend base desires.

Platonic opposite-sex friendships might even be important for our psychological health. Famed psychologist Carl Jung put forth the theory of animus and anima—animus refers to male energy present within females, and anima refers to female energy present with males. Part of the reason we gravitate toward opposite-sex friendships, beyond mating, is to connect with these parts of our personality that balance us.

If you don't agree that men and women can be platonic friends, then the underlying message is that emotion isn't easily separable. Friendship, affection, love, support, and intimacy are all heavily interrelated, so sometimes sex is just a stone's throw away from a close friendship. Friendship itself might arise because there is underlying sexual attraction—in other words, sometimes we become friends with members of the opposite sex as a long-term road to having sex with them.

In 2012, researchers surveyed a group of

heterosexual males and females about their opposite-sex friendships, and the results suggest a combination of the two views is correct (Bleske-Rechek et al., 2012).

For the females, there was a harsh divide. They were able to view a friendship as purely platonic or a romance in waiting. Males, on the other hand, seemed unable to disassociate their opposite-sex friendships from the idea of sex or the possibility of sex with their female friends.

In the same vein, males were more likely than the females to perceive sexual interest from their opposite sex friends, while women perceived the opposite. Men saw signs of a potential sexual relationship embedded everywhere in a friendship, while women reported signs of a platonic relationship everywhere. The women interpreted sexual interest as friendliness, while the men interpreted friendliness as sexual interest. In a purported platonic friendship, this implies that, most of the time, males operate under ulterior sexual motives.

According to this study, the chase may not save you here, at least if you are a male, it seems. If a woman has made up her mind, you may be stuck without a hope.

For males, being "just a friend" almost always has undertones of "a friend that I haven't had sex with yet." This doesn't mean there can't be a flourishing friendship or that the parties can't mutually benefit in huge ways, but it may stun women to learn that many of their male friends are only their friends because they have a pull of sexual attraction to them. It doesn't always mean they want more than friendship, but it does indicate their motives aren't always innocent.

Women don't hold this perspective and appear to be able to whole-heartedly have platonic feelings toward men. It would be easy to throw blame at the evolutionary imperative males have to view every female as a potential child bearer and maximize their opportunities, but I think the reason is much simpler these days. The social dynamics of any party will demonstrate it—males compete for females, while females don't compete as much for men. Simple logic dictates that men are actively surrounding themselves with women that they want to have sex with, while women are not.

Men and women certainly can be great friends, but the impulse that built these friendships can be very different. But if you meet a goal and each party is satisfied with their withdrawal from the relationship bank, does it matter how the goal was met?

Men have friendships based on sexual attraction, regardless of whether it is plausible or fulfilled. A man's friend circle is full of women he is sexually attracted to, but for various reasons he may or may not act on his desires. This shouldn't devalue the friendships; it's just the impetus for seeking them out in the first place. If a male doesn't find a female sexually attractive, it doesn't mean that an amazing friendship cannot blossom. But sexual attraction is a primary motivator for males.

Very rarely do men forego this so-called shallow approach. Women on the other hand appear to view men in a far more holistic manner, and attractiveness by itself is not a significant factor in choosing their opposite sex friends.

Of course, same-sex friendships avoid most of these problems and bring their own special benefits. Relationships between females are fraught with more combined oxytocin, which creates a network of support, intimacy, and empathy that is literally lacking from male bloodstreams (Taylor and Klein, 2000). Male relationships, on the other hand, are somewhat more primitive, much like their view of females as sexual opportunities. Aristotle put it this way:

> *Perfect friendship is the friendship of men who are good, and alike in virtue; for these wish well alike to each other qua good, and they are good themselves… But it is natural that such*

friendships should be infrequent; for such men are rare.

Further, such friendship requires time and familiarity; as the proverb says, men cannot know each other till they have "eaten salt together"; nor can they admit each other to friendship or be friends till each has been found lovable and been trusted by each. Those who quickly show the marks of friendship to each other wish to be friends, but are not friends unless they both are lovable and know the fact; for a wish for friendship may arise quickly, but friendship does not.

The movie *When Harry Met Sally* famously proposed that men and women can be platonic friends with no romantic intentions. It's a romantic comedy so it was inevitable that Billy Crystal and Meg Ryan end up together, but science backs it up completely.

Takeaways:

- The chase is something we subconsciously do, despite outwardly decrying having to play dating games.
- Mostly, the chase has to do with the appeal and addictiveness of intermittent rewards and understanding why human nature works this way.
- The other portion of the chase is about how unavailability is attractive because we immediately begin to ruminate on what we are missing out on and what we are being deprived of.
- However, the chase is not a foolproof method, even though it takes advantage of human psychology. Most of us have been faced with being rejected and told that we are only thought of as friends and not romantic partners. Is there a way to deal with this?
- For females, perhaps. Studies have shown that females do indeed see males platonically, but males do not do the same for females. Can males and females be only platonic friends? Yes, but it will usually be the female's choice.

Chapter 4. All About Flirting

Next time you have a free moment, stand outside an elementary school and watch the children play during recess. Make sure you're not wearing a trench coat and staring for too long, otherwise the teachers will call the police on you.

While you're (surreptitiously) watching the children, take special note of how the little boys and girls interact. They will be flirting in the way only children do, and it will be pretty easy to spot. The boys will pick on the girls and pull their hair; the girls will scream and swat the boys away. The boys will throw soccer balls at the girls; the girls will keep the soccer balls and fold their arms together in sneers. Shins will get kicked, and cooties will be spread.

Adults do the exact same things, just in a subtler manner.

Flirting is the art of getting the attention of the opposite sex—what you use the attention for is up to you. Flirting is undeniably an important part of how we create attraction and get what we want romantically. It allows us to say, "Hey, I'm interested in you," without actually saying it, and sometimes the uncertainty makes the message even stronger.

Just as with any learned behavior, there are more and less effective ways of doing it as adults. Some of us are still stuck in the playground mentality of flirting that I just described. Others of us are flat-out trying to flirt incorrectly. I don't mean there is only one objectively correct way to flirt. Many people try to flirt in a way they have read about, but it isn't compatible with their personality. This obviously will lead to bad outcomes.

They try to be someone they're not, which completely takes away any advantage they may have had. It's like someone who's seven feet tall using the basketball strategies of someone who is five feet tall. The taller person may have read about the shorter person's strategies working, but they probably aren't a good fit for someone who can easily put the ball through the hoop by simply raising their hand. There are specific types of flirting that work best for your personality and how you like to relate to the opposite sex. Take advantage of your unique strengths and quirks, and don't lose yourself trying to conform to what other people might advise you to do.

Five Flirting Styles

A study conducted at the University of Kansas (Hall, 2007) found there are five main types of flirting, and you probably tend to utilize more than one type.

Through your dating odyssey, you've dealt with people who've tried to get their message across in various ways—some successful and some not. Their problem (or yours) was they didn't realize flirting is like improvisational jazz.

There are so many possible directions, and the more jazz scales you know, the better you can play. If you're stuck on one modality or scale, you lack the ability to go where more knowledgeable jazz artists can go. You're limited, and your overall ability for jazz will be seriously restricted. In other words, if you can learn and internalize the difference between alternative types of flirting, the better flirter you will be and the more attractive you will be to the opposite sex.

You might be more comfortable with one type of flirting over others, but understanding the different types and knowing when to use them gives you a tremendous advantage. Here's another reason this matters: if the person you want to flirt with is at all attractive, you are not the only person that desires them. Sometimes dating is simply a horse race—a numbers game. If one of your competitors has three or four tricks up their sleeve while you only have one, you are going to be at a serious disadvantage in winning that person's heart.

In the event you are, for whatever reason, prevented from using your primary method of flirting, what can you do if you don't have a backup method? Will you be able to compensate or cope?

Finally, different people are receptive to different approaches. The more flirting types and methods you know, the higher the likelihood you can connect with someone. You just need to learn to speak everyone's language.

So how can you flirt consistently and successfully? Let's dive into the five types of flirts there are and the methods they use to see how we can better arm ourselves for close-quarters contact.

The five types of flirts are:

1. Physical
2. Polite
3. Playful
4. Sincere
5. Traditional

Physical flirts use their bodies to deliver their message and draw attention to themselves. Instead of using words, they will use nonverbal signals such as sustained eye contact, open body language, and proactive touching to show interest.

They can be subtle, but physical flirts are almost always more aggressive and direct by nature. Let's be honest: this is the kind of flirting that many of us want to use but don't feel comfortable using. It's forward and confident, and it gets you from Point A to Point B in the shortest time possible.

It's also riskier, and rejection is always lurking around the corner, but that also speaks to the physical flirt's level of confidence. They know what they want, they shoot for it, and they are ready to accept the consequences either way.

Physical flirts excel in situations where they have physical freedom and space in which to operate. Sitting down and having dinner is a nightmare date for a physical flirt because there is a literal barrier between the two people and they can't play the way they want to. A physical flirt values someone who is adept at reading body language, not shy with their own body, and is physically affectionate. If they express themselves physically, they can read those signs from others as well.

If this resonates with you, you can be a more effective physical flirt if you can delineate between the three types of touch from the earlier chapter on flirting without speaking. In particular, use the plausible deniability and nuclear types of touch mixed together. You should also put yourself in situations where you have freedom of movement and where incidental contact is likely to occur.

Please be skilled at reading other people, because if you're not, you will make people uncomfortable very quickly.

The *polite flirt* is the type of person you can bring home to meet your mother and father. They flirt conservatively and communicate their interest in a very guarded and nonsexual manner.

They are the opposite of forward and can sometimes come off as inhibited or repressed. But that's not why they move slowly. They just want to assess a situation and know they are making the right choice for themselves. They wait for a situation to unfold as much as possible, then make their decisions based on more complete information. Of course, there are considerable downsides to this.

A polite flirt will accept other people's signs of flirting but not necessarily reciprocate outwardly. They are passive participators in flirting, which means they simply react to and accept the flirting from others. Sometimes the lack of rejection or objection from a polite flirt should be taken as a positive sign of their attraction. They can be difficult to read, so some people may be too discouraged at the lack of positive feedback to continue engaging with a polite flirt. They want to keep their cards close to their chest for any number of reasons.

Polite flirts are most comfortable in situations where conversation is the main activity, such as a coffee date. This allows them to go at their own pace and stay platonic as long as they want. A polite flirt values someone who is willing to take it slow and not focus on sex—perhaps a rarity in this day and age.

If this resonates with you, you can be a more effective polite flirt by being reactive to people and not bending to the social pressure of doing what you *think* you should do. Come to peace with yourself and recognize that you prefer to take things slowly and let everything fall into place. Be aware that you might have to throw people a bone, so to speak, to keep encouraging them to pursue you. And make sure you're not labeling yourself as a polite flirt because you lack confidence to proactively engage others. Put yourself in situations that are almost platonic by nature, and be open to overtures from friends because that is where your romantic relationships might come from.

Finally, be prepared to go through dry spells because you are essentially waiting for others to engage you.

Playful flirts are all about flirting for the sake of flirting. It's one of their favorite pastimes, and they do it without regard to how others may perceive it or even be affected. They'll make sexual overtures not meant to be taken seriously and generally be forward with the assumption that others are in on the joke.

They turn everything into a game, for better or worse, and it's easy to have a good time with them. They're always ready to engage and play around.

If they don't always mean it, then what are their goals with flirting with everyone?

Usually their goal is to create attraction for its own sake. It's not a negative goal, but it might not be a good fit for those who are looking for more meaningful connections. They have a wide social circle and they aren't shy with the opposite sex—but do be aware they might also use flirting to validate their self-esteem.

The playful flirt will be at the center of the room when there is attention to be had, and they enjoy creating and playing with sexual tension. This sounds like a negative perspective of the playful flirt, but it's not negative. The playful flirt just enjoys flirting and will do it whatever the context. From another perspective, they are just planting as many seeds as possible and making dating a true numbers game.

A playful flirt values someone who is willing to engage in games for the sake of it and who doesn't read deeply into situations. They are likely to enjoy easygoing and spontaneous partners. People who are overly serious or sincere in their flirting aren't good matches because there will be constant miscommunication.

If this resonates with you, you can be a more effective playful flirt if you make it clear upfront to others that you enjoy flirting with everyone. That way, no one gets the wrong idea and you don't have to constantly explain yourself. You can also try to identify other playful flirts who would love to engage with you and avoid the other types of flirts who are clearly looking for deeper connections.

The *sincere flirt* is also direct, but they look to express an interest in the other person as a complete being. In other words, the sincere flirt makes their overtures more about their target's emotional, mental, spiritual, and physical attraction.

They enjoy creating sexual tension, but they also seek to connect in emotional and spiritual ways. Where to the playful flirt a flirtatious conversation might be centered on sex, a flirtatious conversation to the sincere flirt might be centered around spiritual beliefs or emotional needs.

Another way this is different than playful flirting is because playful flirts aim to make others feel good on a shallow, playful level, and the sincere flirt is trying to hit a deeper emotional note to build upon. They get personal and deep fast, and to some, this can feel invasive. It can be classified as an intense type of flirtation.

Sincere flirts have fun, but first and foremost, they focus on building deep rapport and emotional connection—things that can be truly terrifying to some. They run the risk of injecting a serious, heavy atmosphere in an otherwise light and adventurous back-and-forth exchange with the person they would like to establish a relationship with.

Sincere flirts do best in goal-oriented situations with clear outcomes. They don't play games and don't accept them. A sincere flirt values someone who shares the same values, communicates well, and wants mental intimacy. If you meet that threshold, you'll be taken seriously, and if you don't, you might be quickly dropped.

If this resonates with you, you can be a more effective sincere flirt if you make it explicit upfront that you are looking for something deeper and more serious. This will help you filter who you spend your precious time on. Additionally, because you may have a penchant for scaring others off, you can formulate indirect ways to initially connect with people emotionally and spiritually to build rapport.

Traditional flirts embrace gender roles. What exactly does this mean?

If you are a male, you are likely to fulfill what you feel is the typical male gender role of taking control, being chivalrous, planning everything, and generally being a gentleman. If you are a woman, you will fulfill the corresponding female gender role and be more passive and reactive, and you'll allow yourself to be chased and catered to. Think of how a 1950s man would court a 1950s woman and you have the dynamic of the traditional flirt.

Traditional flirts are the likeliest to let men lead while women take a more passive role. Traditional flirting is a very male-centered form of flirting. It is like a dance where the man leads and chases. As an acquaintance put it very directly, "Back in the old day, when men wanted to show their interest, they sent you flowers. If you didn't reply, they just sent *more* flowers!"

The downside is when you encounter someone who (1) pictures themselves as a traditional flirt but is not or (2) pictures themselves as the opposite of a traditional flirt, but is actually traditional. They cause massive confusion because they feel social pressure to be one way or the other and send mixed messages to everyone involved. These people are in effect hiding their real intentions because of how they've been told they should date.

A traditional flirt values someone who doesn't mind gender roles and is willing to play their part. They don't see them as backward, old-fashioned, or pigeonholing—they see a natural divide in female and male energy and don't mind acting upon it. In fact, it makes them feel empowered and attractive because they have a clear guideline for how they should act.

If this resonates with you, all you have to do is act on your instincts and you will naturally filter out those who have more traditional views on dating. Some people might be offended by your so-called old-fashioned notions, but that doesn't mean you should change them. After all, some people like soccer and some people like baseball—it doesn't mean one group is worse or incorrect.

What's notable is that these five styles are all across the board, but they have the exact same goal: to engineer attraction and feelings of love. There are multiple ways of getting to the same goal?

This forces us to ask two questions. First, which styles resonate with you and which can you wield with most effectiveness? Second, what do the people you want to flirt with respond to the best?

Imagine how much more effective you will be if you discover what works best for you while simultaneously understanding how someone else likes to be engaged with? Without this type of knowledge, it's almost as if you're going in blind and winging it and expecting success—which is unreasonable to expect given the circumstances. It's common that people think they are great at conveying their attraction to someone—and maybe they are, but only in one style of flirting, to one type of flirter.

Your chosen style of flirting just might be hampering your romantic overtures in more ways than one, as the next section proves.

The Stages of Flirting

When was the last time you were out at a bar or club at closing time?

If you were sober and took a look around, you might have observed some very interesting aspects of human mating. This is the stage of the night when people want to seal the deal and move from the bar to someone's bed. More aggressive acts are taken, and *Hail Marys* are thrown. Some people are consistently successful, while others almost always go home alone.

Why is that? Is it really just that some of us are that much more charming, or is there something going on in the background they have tapped into?

The scientifically proven answer lies within *scripts*. People follow scripts for pretty much everything they engage in, from ordering at a restaurant to going to the doctor's office.

For example, at Burger King, you know someone is going to ask for your order, ask if you want a drink with it, and then you will pay them. After you pay them, you will get a receipt and then be pointed to an area where you wait for your food. That's just one of many scripts we know and are familiar with in our daily lives. It means that you know exactly how to act in that situation, you know what to expect, you know what stage you're at, and you know what you're missing. It allows you to consistently be successful there. Waiting for the cashier to give you the receipt and your order number is almost instinctual. You don't think about it because it's a script you've engaged in countless times.

It shouldn't be a surprise, then, that going from strangers to flirting to the possibility of sex has a script as well, a script that makes it easy to escalate from one stage to the next because of how familiar it all seems. It's just not a script that we have known explicitly, until 1980 when Timothy Perper and Susan Fox studied and determined the exact stages of successful flirtation to sex.

Knowing this script is more important than you might think. Just as you know the script for success at Burger King, knowing the script that Perper and Fox discovered will show you methods for successful flirting, period. You will be able to see what you are missing, what you may have skipped, what you still need to do, and, overall, how to achieve your goal of sex via flirting. You should also integrate this knowledge with the previous section's discovery of your flirting style to see how you might be falling short.

The researchers sat in singles bars and watched people who entered alone and ended up leaving with other people at the end of the night. In other words, these were people who started as strangers, then utilized flirting as a means to sex. They discovered three main stages in the script for successful flirtation of those who more often than not left with someone for the night.

The stages are:

1. Approach
2. Synchronize
3. Touch

We'll go through each in more detail so you can see exactly what's involved in a successful flirtation interaction, no matter the style of flirting.

The first stage is the approach stage. As you might guess, this governs how a successful approach of a stranger for flirtation works. If the approach is not received warmly or at all, the flirtation will immediately end.

So what is involved in a successful approach that would culminate in a higher chance of sexual intercourse? The researchers articulated three distinct points that would predict how well an approach would go.

The first factor was the direction and orientation of the approach. Males disliked being approached from the front, but females disliked being approached from the side (Fisher & Byrne, 1975). This speaks to how the different genders felt about violations of personal space. Males felt more comfortable being approached from the side, whereas females felt more comfortable being approached from the front. This means females actually felt more comfortable with a greater degree of violation of their personal space. Males tended to welcome directness, while females wanted to first feel more secure and less threatened. Choose the wrong orientation and the first stage is set up for failure.

The second factor is smiles. The researchers found that the more each party smiled, the more a successful approach was likely to have occurred. It didn't matter whether the participants approached with a joke or even a serious conversation topic. The smile indicated an emotional arousal, interest on a party's behalf, and the willingness to show that interest to the other person. Of note, only genuine smiles were indicative; an insincere smile was characterized by being delayed, a lack of eye wrinkles, and a lack of teeth shown.

The final factor that determined a successful approach was people's use of their eyebrows and overall facial expressiveness. When we use our eyebrows separately and independently from other nonverbal gestures, we are essentially conveying interest with them. The researchers called this "flashing" our eyebrows. Using eyebrow flashes was more successful when approaching the opposite sex and led to people being able to continue along the script.

Synchronization. This is the second stage to a successful flirtation interaction and will only occur when the first stage of approaching was successful. Of course, the script is sequential because the so-called prospect must feel additional levels of warmth and comfort in order for the end goal to come to fruition.

Once the actual physical approach is accepted or welcomed, then a conversation must begin.

Other various studies have expounded on what types of pickup lines work best. The ones that worked best in the flirtation context were not cute and flippant. Trying too hard to be clever had a higher chance of failure. What worked more consistently, and was reported to generate higher levels of interest, were simple, straightforward introductions or observations about the environment. In other words, keep it simple, stupid. An effective pickup line, or some kind of conversation starter, is important because it's what leads to quick synchronization.

The reason this stage is called "synchronize" is because people's bodies will literally synchronize to face each other, and their movements and energy will become similar so as to adjust and adapt to the other person. That's what happens when you participate in an engaging conversation with someone you hold in high regard. When rapport and interest are established, we begin mirroring their tone of voice and body language in an effort to appear more similar, and thus attractive, to them.

A successful synchronization stage is characterized by people simply looking directly at each other, making eye contact, being physically close, and appearing engaged. Both parties have signaled that they are interested in a continuing interaction by locking their positions. Initial attraction has been built, and they pass each other's superficial filters and first impressions. They're speaking, but they're also analyzing each other's body language and facial expressions to determine the level of interest they should show.

This is where the flirtation game truly begins—it's a subtle test of how attracted you really are to the other person. After physical synchronization, physical touch begins.

Touch. At this point, both physical and mental attraction has been established, and it's time to escalate. This is the final stage of a successful flirtation interaction: if the parties successfully touch each other, and the touch is received warmly, then the feedback will spur the parties to touch each other more, and the rest is history.

Of course, this stage isn't only about touch.

It's about the continued rapport and tension that is created as a result of being in close proximity with each other. Touching heightens that and makes intentions clearer. Both parties will start at more neutral touching that can be interpreted in multiple ways before diving into the types of touch that are unmistakable in their intent and purpose. Breaking the touch barrier can feel electric.

If the touch barrier has been crossed and accepted by both parties, the script comes to an end because there is nowhere else to escalate to—in public, at least. You might differ on the path you took to get here, but this script was observed to be highly effective. The three stages of flirting that Perper and Fox found aren't a guarantee of sex, but if you make sure to hit these stages, you will set yourself up for success.

Now that we know the stages of flirting to sex, what should we do with this knowledge? We need to diagnose how we send out our own messages, what we are doing, and what we aren't doing.

For example, many people think they make their intentions well known, but they never so much as touch their intended mates. Clearly, that's something to address because they are not following the flirting script that has been proven to be effective and successful.

Others may skip right over the approach phase and immediately begin touching. That's too aggressive and forward for most people. What the script actually defines is the process of building rapport and comfort with strangers. Turns out it functions the same at networking events as it does for flirting and sex.

This script is highly simplified, but that's about as good as you can get for human interaction. There are so many shades of gray and different interpretations of the same action that three steps are as good of a guideline as you are going to get.

This allows us to visualize what we should be

doing or what we should be looking for. If you want to approach a stranger, you should make sure that your actual physical approach is improved and smooth and that you have a conversation starter immediately ready to employ. Then, after building rapport with humor, you should begin touching to create a sense of tension and attraction. Don't skip ahead, and don't neglect a step thinking that you are above it or don't need it. It's been scientifically proven that you're not so special that you don't!

If some of this sounds clinical, it's because to some degree, it is. Humans study the behavior of rats by adjusting variables and administering more cheese or shocks. Human patterns of behavior can be studied in essentially the same way. The sex drive is one of the most powerful human motivators, and in a sense, can make us predictable sometimes. Flirting is to running through mazes, and the possibility of sex is to cheese if you were to continue along that analogy.

Understand your flirting style, and then

understand how it fits, or doesn't fit, into the stages of flirting that have been observed to work. And no kicking of shins.

Takeaways:

- Flirting is hard to define, but in general, the goal is to gain someone's attention and make it known that you are interested in them. There are many ways to do this, but not everything will work for everyone.
- Hence, researchers have articulated five distinct flirting styles: physical, polite, traditional, playful, and sincere. It's important to ask what you can use best and what your paramour will best respond to. Having more tools in your tool bag is always a good thing.
- Researchers have additionally discovered a three-step process people who were successful in leaving with someone from bars used consistently. The three steps are approach, synchronize, and touch. It's important to analyze what you are doing, what you are not doing, and if you are skipping over a step or staying on one too

long. You should also consider how your flirting style fits into this process.

Chapter 5. Love Is All That Matters...

Arranged marriages are a spin on love that hasn't quite made the jump to the so-called Western world. To most people in Western cultures, the notion fundamentally redefines the entire purpose of marriage in a less than positive way.

In the West, marriage is about freedom, choice, and ultimately love. An arranged marriage, at least from a superficial standpoint, involves values that are the mirror opposite of liberty and diversity of options. Love is entirely about emotional connection and chemistry, so how can you reduce it to an arrangement where the participants don't even meet each other until weeks or days before their wedding?

When parents in traditional Asian cultures, Indian in particular, arrange marriages for their children, they factor in compatibility and long-term prospects. It will better inform the rest of this chapter if we first take a look at how the Indian matchmaking and arranged marriage process works. I took it upon myself to perform due diligence and survey over a dozen Indian couples who had arranged marriages, as well as an Indian matchmaker.

The Process

Let's take two single individuals, Neha and Kunal, who live in Mumbai, India.

They are both nearing 26 years old, and their parents decide they now need to take charge and help their children start their own families. They each have great careers with much upside potential, and it's only natural that they move to the next level in terms of their relationships.

Note that it's a decision their parents and family make, because that's exactly who tends to take the lead in securing spouses for their children. In many cases, young Indian adults rely entirely on their parents and family for this part of their life and only make fledgling attempts at romance themselves before they begin the process with their parents. They may even view arranged marriages as a pleasant fallback to depend on.

Indian arranged marriages are approached by the parents and families like a business decision first and foremost. Both sets of parents will shine a beacon into the community and ask their friends and acquaintances if they know anyone suitable for their child, all the while selling their virtues like a beautiful piece of pottery.

Neha's and Kunal's parents have a mutual friend with whom they attended university, and that friend has made both sets of parents aware that there was a single young adult of the opposite sex who seemed like a good match on paper. That is, they were close in age, their families had similar standing and finances, and, most important, Neha and Kunal were both sufficiently acceptable (if not impressive) to the other person's parents. In essence, we're talking about a matchmaker.

The parents were put in touch, details were ironed out and confirmed, and then pictures were sent along for approval to Neha's and Kunal's families. Kunal was a bit more enthused than Neha by the pictures, but both agreed to meet the following week.

Neha and Kunal met at a café for about two hours, but it probably didn't resemble any date you've been on. Both sets of parents wanted to come, but Neha and Kunal wanted to be a bit more modern about it. Their meeting was fairly serious and more like a discussion about whether a business partnership would be appropriate. They discussed long-term goals, values, shared morals, and questions designed to determine how they felt about certain issues.

When would children be expected? Would one party be expected to give up their career for child-rearing? Where did they want to live and what kind of lifestyle did they have? What's their perspective on religion?

They ended the date with a handshake and went home with their parents to discuss how it went.

With their parents, they discussed all the answers and how they might play out; nothing was left to chance. If the "date" and the post-date discussion with their parents went extremely well, the couple might not even meet again before agreeing to marry and notifying each other of their intent, but more commonly they would meet two or three more times before making their final decision. There would be no proposal per se.

Because the truly important factors that determine compatibility and fit (though not love) are discussed honestly and openly, combined with an extremely high degree of commitment, the marriage is deemed to have an extremely high chance of success.

There can be no better evidence for this other than how lavish and extravagant Indian weddings are by design. The groom traditionally rides in on a white horse at the head of a caravan. Guest lists can number into the thousands, and it's not uncommon for people to sell homes or other large assets in order to have the funds to finance the type of wedding they want for their child.

Keep in mind that this is a more modern version of Indian arranged marriages—back in the olden days, the bride and groom might only have met for the first time at the altar.

As you can see, in an arranged marriage, love plays no role whatsoever in the final decision. Nowhere in the description of that process was affection even mentioned. If they happened to have some chemistry, that would be icing on the cake, but it's not seen as a prerequisite to marriage.

But What About Love?

Indeed, what about love?

What is love's role in arranged marriage? Love marriages, as they are referred to in India, are driven by connection and chemistry while family, values, and lifestyle are often drowned out and completely ignored. Phrased in this light, it's almost too easy to see why there are so many bumps in Western marriages, and that the current (2017) rate of divorce is roughly 30% according to data from the National Survey of Family Growth.

The Western idea of compatibility has long been confined to elusive chemistry, with total disregard for practicality.

It's not taken into account per se, but the belief is that once the big factors involving values and worldviews are accounted for, love that starts with familiarity will take care of itself and slowly evolve. Love is seen as something that grows over time as a function of a few things.

First, the *proximity effect*, which is a psychological phenomenon in which people who share the same proximity tend to like each other more and more. There have been studies conducted in which subjects rated people more favorably merely because they spent more time with them or because they had been physically closer to them. It's why we have a certain type of affection for our neighbors, the baristas we see every morning, or the odd person on the bus you see weekly.

With the proximity effect, arranged marriages find suitable matches in every respect minus love, and love and affection can grow between any two people living and working together in close proximity.

Second, people who consent to arranged unions also place a high premium on commitment. This plays a tremendous role in how well the marriage fares in the future.

Francine Kaye, a relationship and marriage

expert, had this to say on commitment in arranged marriages:

> *It should be pointed out that arranged marriages work because culturally marriage is seen differently. We have a very romantic view of marriage. Theirs is more pragmatic... In the West marriages are easy to get out of. But in arranged marriages, the commitment is very strong. They get married knowing they won't leave, so when times are harder—if they face injury or trauma—they don't run away. It brings them closer.*

When a partner looks at the marriage more like a partnership or business relationship, they put more focus into making it work. They don't see leaving or divorce as an option and are thus committed to solving issues and compromise. This tendency to look into the future and get around problems before they appear gives arranged marriages a strategic advantage that passion-based relationships do not have.

You're solving problems with solutions that should last 50 years, so what actions will you take to make it work? It's going to be significantly different. People who get into arranged marriages do not look at passion or any short-term consideration. Rather, they look at whether they are going to have children, the quality of the education of those children, and other factors that look way into the future. They also look at retirement and growing old together.

There is an emphasis on problem-solving and conflict skills, which studies have also confirmed is a primary indicator of marriage longevity and happiness.

Marriages, despite what some people might present to the outside world, are never conflict-free lovefests. Even with the best of friends and lovers, there are bound to be fights. When you spend most of your day with someone, logic dictates that you don't agree 100% on everything. In fact, you can look at it this way: if you agree on 80% of matters, that's just a rounding error from 100% because 100% doesn't exist.

So when you hit a bump in the road, do you handle it or sweep it under the rug? If you sweep it under the rug, it will fester and leak out in the form of passive-aggressive behavior before turning into full-out bitterness and resentment? If you choose to address it, are you doing so in a way that will lead to a solution and not further entrenchment?

More successful and happy couples have open lines of communication. They can more easily deal with such issues in a productive manner because they don't overreact or inject emotion into the issue. Their focus on commitment makes them focus on being solution-oriented. If you imagine that your marriage is indeed forever and for life, then you might as well attempt to find a solution as soon as possible instead of suffering with your problem for decades.

On a related note, there's the simple expectation that it's going to take work. Nothing will be easy, and you can't simply sweep it under the rug. If you barely know someone, you know you will need to invest considerable effort, and this is the type of

effort most "love" marriages don't have—
because they don't necessarily see the need
to. It's amazing the difference expectations
can make.

It may sound unromantic and clinical, but a
series of studies by Harvard's Dr. Robert
Epstein led him to conclude, based on a series
of tests on romantic love and passion
developed by Elaine Hatfield and Susan
Sprecher, that feelings of passionate and
romantic love are only at about half-capacity
after 18 months in a relationship. It's not
unreasonable to project that after three or
four years, those feelings are considerably
more withered.

Meanwhile, love in arranged marriages
appears to grow gradually and linearly and
actually surpasses the levels of love in love
marriages at about the five-year point. He
also found that after 10 years together, the
affection in arranged marriages is twice as
strong as that in love marriages—because of
the matching values and similarities.

Additional studies were conducted at the University of Rajasthan with the same conclusion. Love marriages under one year old averaged a score of 70 out of 91 on a love scale, and the numbers fell consistently over time. After 10 years, they had an average score of 40. Arranged marriages under one year old averaged a score of 58 out of 91. Yet, after 10 years, they scored an average of 68. Arranged marriages might start lower, but on a long-term basis, they might indeed produce happier and healthier marriages.

It's not a stretch to say that compatibility is about much more than chemistry and connection, both of which are destined to fade. The message underlying these differences with arranged marriages is that attraction comes as a byproduct of commitment, proximity, and problem-solving. It sounds a bit more like a relationship with coworkers.

And love marriages? Well, Epstein sums it up well:

The idea is we must not leave our love lives to chance. We plan our education, our careers and our finances but we're still uncomfortable with the idea that we should plan our love lives. I do not advocate arranged marriages but I think a lot can be learned from them.

It's not the fairytale that we've been sold since our childhood, but since when has that been realistic? I'm not sure I see Cinderellas and Snow Whites roaming around the streets.

When you're mating and dating, focus on presenting how you two fit together in a business sense, just like the Indian process emphasizes. Everyone likes to be able to see the long-term view and how everything will work out years down the road, so if you can make that more salient and obvious, you will be more attractive in a logical manner.

Love or Similarity?

We've taken a look at how love can take a back seat to problem-solving skills and a simple commitment to work and investment.

Here's another proposition: love may also be less important than how *similar* you are to your potential mate.

Would you want to date someone with the same traits and interests as you, or someone who is different but *complementary*?

It's one of the questions we've asked ourselves multiple times without even realizing it. When we meet someone new, we instinctively wonder how we'll fit together. Is it going to be two identical puzzle pieces, or are you going to be two puzzle pieces that fit together to complete the picture? Do you need someone that thinks in the exact same way as you, or do you need someone who complements your weaknesses and balances you out?

Conventional wisdom (something that people repeat enough so that it seems that it should be true) dictates that opposites attract. And at first glance, there is wisdom in this idea. Opposites can smooth each other's flaws and make each other stronger in areas where they are weak. We admire people who can do things we cannot, so naturally we like our opposites at times. The whole is stronger than the sum of its parts.

Opposites can be complementary to us and introduce us to an entirely different world. It can be a thrilling challenge and take us outside of our comfort zones to grow as people. Things are novel and exciting every day. Besides, when you've just started dating someone, the honeymoon period effect is fairly strong and you overlook most things. Who's to say that initially you would pay attention to how similar or different you two are?

The thing you might find adorable and endearing just might be the same thing that drives you up the wall after the honeymoon period. So what happens after the relationship is past that glorious honeymoon period? This is where conventional wisdom hits some rough spots. When the novelty dies, you're left with two people who share completely different values.

There is a reason why, in survey after survey, successful couples in long-term relationships tend to be flat-out similar (Kaufman, 2011). Studies have even shown that couples that *look more alike* physically tend to be happier and in longer relationships.

Many people make the mistake of believing that their dissimilar interests and values will intertwine at some point. This is essentially the belief that you or your partner will fundamentally change. For example, that the other person will change or that you will eventually be able to change their minds about foundational beliefs that are tied to their identity. How many marriages have ended over the fact that one party wanted children, the other didn't, and both thought the other would eventually change?

How many people have wished for their partner to convert religions or political positions for them but are upset when neither party wishes to change? When both parties believe the other person will change, it means they themselves aren't willing to, and the chance of a compromise is even lower. Values don't change as a result of osmosis or proximity. They're deep-seated and, even with effort, can't easily change. The same goes for interests.

According to the studies, truly successful couples tended to have similar interests when their relationship started, and they bonded over their similarity. They liked to do similar things and shared similar views on important issues.

Their similarity may even have been the impetus for their relationship beginning because it caused one of the parties to lower their guard and be open to the other. There's a fairly strong evolutionary basis for preferring similarity. We were more likely to survive if we stuck to shapes, shadows, and sounds we recognized versus unfamiliar ones that could be saber-toothed tigers lurking in the shadows.

There's also a very human element to

similarity. What if you met someone and you discovered that you grew up just minutes away from each other in the same tiny town in another country? You're going to automatically see them in another light and be more open to them, and this can be the beginning of a romantic relationship.

So opposites do *attract*, but to finish the quote, opposites then *attack*. The factors that set you apart will eventually bubble to the surface. We have to tackle the inconvenient reality that pairings involving opposite personalities tend to break up more frequently (Hudson & Fraley, 2014).

Let's indulge in stereotypes.

An artisan performer can be drawn to a rational banker and vice versa. The banker can be drawn to the performer because the performer is socially driven, gregarious, loves to live loudly, and is very optimistic. The performer can be drawn to the banker because they are organized, cautious, fun to make fun of, and a realist.

These differences in temperament, which are polar opposites, help complete both personalities. Both parties feel they are more complete individuals within the relationship. But the seeds of destruction have also been planted.

The rational banker is very big on money management and personal responsibility. The artisan, on the other hand, is not very good with money or time management. The banker's cold personality orientation can lead to the artisan feeling shut out and as if defensive walls are up. The artisan is extremely spontaneous and carefree, while the banker must plan things days in advance (and not only because their job has long and demanding hours).

Sooner or later, that relationship will go on life support, sustaining it long after it should have naturally ended. The culprits here are the deep and fundamental differences in the personality orientations of the partners.

Both partners need to be honest regarding their own needs and those of their partner's—sometimes you just can't fulfill them because you are too different. Usually, people don't change for others. They are mostly incapable of it, and that's okay. The best they can do is alter their behavior to appease their significant other. And although that is important, it's also ephemeral and therefore temporary—though not for lack of trying or absence of desire to accommodate.

A lot of heartache and fertile years could be saved if we internalized this fact of life. People usually can't or don't change who they are at their core. We all want to be the exception to the rule, but that's statistically just not reasonable or possible.

What does this mean for your relationship? You have to try to suss out whether someone is really trying to change or just appeasing you with token actions. The former is a far stronger motivation, but unfortunately it's not easy for people themselves to tell what is driving them—a desire to change or a desire to avoid negative consequences from you.

In a study on whether couples that were more similar in personality were happier than couples that were less similar, subjects rated their own personalities while their partners did the same. They rated their personality based on five metrics, which are generally known as the "big five" of personality traits based on additional studies.

The traits are:

1. Extraversion: how much engagement with the outside world is preferred
2. Conscientiousness: how structured and disciplined one is
3. Openness: willingness to do things that are novel, new, and out of their comfort zone
4. Agreeableness: empathy, trust, and consideration for others
5. Emotional stability (or neuroticism): the ability to be emotionally unreactive and able to cope with negativity

After they rated their personalities, they also completed a questionnaire assessing how happy they were in their current relationship. The results were surprising given the thrust of this chapter.

Of the five personality factors, there were only two that mattered in relationship satisfaction: *agreeableness* and *emotional stability*. The other three factors, extraversion, conscientiousness, and openness, did not need to be similar for a happy relationship.

This might not be surprising if you consider that agreeableness and emotional stability are the two personality factors that could plausibly define compromise and how you might gracefully disagree and have arguments. The other three factors don't take others into account.

Love matters. Or does it? Is it a social construct that has been sold to us via romantic comedies and Disney movies with dashing princes? Or is it something that is the subject of misplaced hopes and dreams?

Takeaways:

- Love is what most of us marry for, but arranged marriages have been around for a very long time. In fact, what most of us would consider romantic love is a luxury that is only a few hundred years old.
- Arranged marriages work precisely because love is placed as a low priority. Instead, commitment, problem-solving, and lowered expectations take the forefront and create conditions that allow for a harmonious relationship to first blossom, which allows love to follow.
- Another factor that appears to be more important than love In relationships is similarity. Studies have shown that similarity is more important because people don't tend to change, and over time, you're just left with conflicting values and worldviews.
- A study specified the traits that predicted the most relationship success if similar: agreeableness and emotional stability.

Chapter 6. Diagnose Yourself

One of the themes throughout this book is just how differently people view attraction and how people bring their own experiences and context to it. There's no one-size-fits-all approach, even to things you think would be universally loved, like giving flowers.

Scenario one: you bring flowers to your paramour, and they love them because flowers remind them of their deceased mother who used to decorate the family home every week with flowers from the farmer's market. Their favorite flowers are carnations, because those were their mother's favorite flowers.

Scenario two: you bring flowers to your paramour, and they stifle the immediate reaction to throw them into the trash. Flowers are the willful killing of an organism for no purpose other than to decorate a home, which is tantamount to murder. That means a flower vase is just a cemetery. On top of it, they have an undisclosed allergy to pollen and immediately begin sneezing on seeing the flowers.

What seemed like a slam dunk was anything but. How we react to an action, of course, says more about us than the action itself. We are all compendiums of experiences that inform our worldviews for better or worse.

What about something else that seems like it would convey a message of love, like wanting to meet the other person's parents?

Scenario one: "That sounds great. I'm glad you seem committed to taking things to the next level. I've told them all about you, and I can't wait for you to meet them!"

Scenario two: "Why? I'm not close to my family and I wouldn't listen to their opinion anyway. My life is my own, and my love life is not something I share with them."

It's a fact that is pretty obvious when we think about it—there are infinite interpretations for any one of your acts. People bring their own experiences, traumas, and associations into their relationships, so you can never be sure that you are conveying exactly what you meant to.

And that's doubly risky in the world of love, where it's often a very precise and pinpointed message you want to convey. Whether it's been while you're dating or to a partner of over 10 years, have you ever done something magnificent and grand for them (like bought them a new car) only to be met with a weakly mustered smile and a less-than-enthusiastic thank-you?

It's likely your partner isn't incredibly dense

or ridiculously callous, so what is going on when something like that happens? Why did they seem to forsake your grand gesture?

Are they just spoiled and taking you for granted? Again, probably not.

The most likely culprit is that you have different *love languages*, a concept pioneered by Gary Chapman in his books and studies.

Love Languages

A love language is how someone demonstrates and perceives affection from someone else. For example, you might show your love and appreciation with a hug and a kiss, while others might show similar feelings by taking you out to dinner. The concept of love languages is predicated on the fact that we express our happiness, pleasure, affection, and love in different ways.

If you bought your partner a new car for your anniversary and they gave a lukewarm reaction, it's not that they don't appreciate the gesture or the car itself. They aren't simply being a spoiled, entitled brat. It's likely that gifts just aren't their love language. Gifts aren't what they value, so their ensuing emotional reaction will reflect that. The same person might be overjoyed if you simply cooked dinner for them on a consistent basis.

Put another way, it's like giving a soccer player a pair of expensive swim goggles. It's a nice gift, but goggles are for swimmers. The soccer player may be appreciative but also think, "Great, what now?" It's just not the soccer player's currency, and though they recognize the gesture, the impact isn't quite there.

If you are flirting with someone that has a different love language from you, it's easy for them to overlook the significance of your gestures and subsequently for you to feel slighted and taken for granted.

This might be okay with small gestures of affection or once in a while, but if this happens with any frequency and in reaction to grand gestures of love, the differences in love languages can quickly take a toll. You begin to feel supremely ignored, belittled, and worthless.

Love languages are crucial to maintaining relationships, but they affect everything in the courtship and flirting phases as well. If you get your wires crossed in how you flirt with somebody, they might mistake your intentions because that's not how they process affection. People make these mistakes constantly. Men give flowers to women who couldn't care less about flowers, and women bake cookies for men who don't eat sweets. Intentions are wonderful all around, and the love is expressed, but not in the ways that will make the most impact to the recipients. If the intent of flirting and acts of romance is to get into someone's good graces, they might not work if love languages aren't understood or aligned.

There are main ways love languages can help you. First, be clear on *your* love languages so you be more self-aware with what matters to you. Second, be clear on the love languages of the people you are with so you can make your intentions and efforts clear. Just as you would not speak Japanese to a French person who only speaks French, you would not use acts of service to communicate your affection to somebody who prefers a comforting touch and vice versa.

The five love languages are:

1. Words of affirmation
2. Quality time
3. Gift-giving
4. Acts of service
5. Physical touch

Most people fall in-between different combinations of these love languages, so don't rule out that you might fall into each language, just in varying degrees. It's not a black or white condition; you can respond to different love languages but prefer one over the others.

Words of affirmation. People who prefer this

love language like to show affection verbally, and they also seek verbal affirmation and praise from their partner.

They prefer verbal affirmations of affection and love over actions, touch, and even sex. This completely turns the traditional idea of actions speaking louder than words on its head. The act of confirmation and validation is what makes them feel.

To people with this love language, hearing praise or love from their partner energizes them and makes them feel more secure in their relationship. Hearing the words "I love you" is more important than grand gestures of love. As you might expect, people with this love language are very verbal. They don't shy away from praise or any type of emotional talk and want the same back from their partner. It's how they feel connected and attractive.

There are a few main ways to use this love language.

You can use encouraging words, the kinds that allow others to find inner strength in difficult times. These words impart courage, belief, trust, and empowerment.

Their own lack of strength or courage could be due to a past traumatic experience or limiting belief. Whatever it is, they lack that fire in their belly that allows them to step up to a challenge, look at it straight in the eye, and take care of business. Encouraging words give people verbal cues that remind them of their potential. You are refocusing their attention from their past failures or inner doubts to the fact that they possess the raw ingredients for success and achievement.

This can be as simple as saying, "Good job" or "You can do it!"

You can use kind words, which are words that communicate love and affection. "I love you," or "This is what I love about you."

You can give compliments—but you knew this one already. You can acknowledge and validate their opinions, stories, and values. You can offer emotional support and respect.

Overall, be more verbal than you think you should be. The easy way to start is to think out loud more and put your thoughts into words. You don't have to view a compliment or words of affection as cheesy or unnecessary if you can just make them daily observations; for example, "That shirt looks great on you" or "You are so good at that, I don't know what I would do without you!" It doesn't come natural for many of us, so it's a matter of creating a habit out of injecting positivity into your everyday life. If this isn't your love language, you might think that each statement is unnecessary and patronizing, but it's some people's number one currency.

Quality time. This is not necessarily *quantity* of time. Quality time is uninterrupted, focused time spent with your partner in a way that allows you to emotionally connect and converse. It can be just 15 minutes, or it can be three hours. The important part is what happens during that time.

If that sounds like a heavy burden, you can simplify it to just having a date where you both leave your phones at home about once a week (or more).

Quality time in raw terms is about the emotional impact and presence of being mentally and emotionally available to your loved ones. It is the opportunity to check in through all aspects, and you can think of it like a checkup at the relationship doctor. It is not measured by where you are. Instead, its quality arises from your emotional presence and the ability to walk away from the time feeling love and presence.

If you are spending time in the same house with your family or your partner, but you are busy answering the phone, doing household chores, or running errands together, that's not quality time. That's the thinking of someone whose love language is *not* quality time. That kind of interaction feels shallow and useless because it's the same type of interaction they might have with a coworker they disdain.

Similarly, you might actually be in a very tightly enclosed space like a bedroom, but if you are both on your phones, it's not quality time.

Engaged and focused attention is the key because you are willfully ignoring other people and obligations and carving out time just for them. You are prioritizing them above everything else. It is how people with this love language feel validated and connected to their partners.

If this doesn't come naturally to you, you can try starting with just 10 minutes. If you put everything aside for 10 minutes and completely focus on what your partner has to say and dive deep in a short period of time, that might be all that's necessary to energize and validate them. Call it a *blitzkrieg* method where the goal is to give your partner extremely intense quality time in short bursts. Remember how attentive you were when you first start dating?

Compare that situation with spending four hours with somebody while you're both fooling around answering emails, chatting with friends, or reading blog articles on yoga.

Hopefully it's becoming clear why it's so important to understand the different love languages. These are completely different motivations and ways of expressing yourself that most people will never differentiate between. At this point, I hope you are also beginning the process of diagnosing yourself and your partner so you will know exactly what will get the best response in the future.

The love languages are exclusively about the other person. It doesn't matter if we think something is a grand gesture or impressive gift; if it doesn't impress the person you intend it to impress, what's the point besides inflating your own ego?

Gift-giving. For many individuals, nothing shows your level of affection and emotional commitment more than your willingness and eagerness to give small gifts.

It's almost never about the gift itself; it's about the implication that they are always on your mind, especially when you are away from each other. It's something you didn't have to do, but you did it anyway because you cared so much about that other person. You can't get them out of your mind, and here is the concrete proof!

Small gifts and tokens show emotional commitment, dedication, and mental and emotional fixation.

Keep in mind that gifts do not have to cost money. In fact, in many contexts, once money enters the equation, it cheapens the emotional value of the gift. People with this love language focus on the thought behind the gift, not the gift itself or its cost.

If you want to spend money, it can be something as cheap as picking up their favorite candy while you're grocery shopping. You can send them a picture of a funny dog you saw. You can draw something for them. You can carve a tiny likeness of them out of a piece of wood. It can be a hat or eye patch for their favorite stuffed animal. It can be a temporary tattoo of their favorite sports team.

Here's a free tip—always have a small gift prepurchased and close at hand if you want to brighten someone's day. With this love language, more gifts are better, but only because they demonstrate how much you are thinking about someone.

For people who don't share this love language, this can seem wasteful and inefficient if you're just giving them clutter or things that will collect dust. But again, it's not about how *you* feel about giving them; it's purely about how the other person feels about receiving the gifts.

It can literally be anything because gifts are a measure of attention and love. It is tangible proof the other person is thinking of them. Write a card or even draw a picture. The value arises from the thought, attention, and focus being made manifest by the gift-giver.

Acts of service. This love language involves doing things that are important to the object of your affection.

For example, if your partner likes very clean surroundings and they see you picking up a broom and cleaning up parts of the house, they will feel loved because they know you are doing it for them. Similarly, if your partner needs help with something work-related and you volunteer to go to the post office for them, that will light up their day.

Acts of service send the message that you are sacrificing your time and energy for them. You are making your life more difficult in order to make their lives easier; you are pitching in as a true partner or teammate does. It's the implication that you see the two of you as a unit and want mutual success.

It's also the implication that you actually understand what is valuable and important to them. Of course, this is the opposite of the words of affirmation love language. Many people can talk a good game and pay lip service to what they should do, or they can just give encouraging words while they sit on the couch doing nothing.

People can say all sorts of things and not really mean them or intend to help out. When you actually perform things that indicate you truly love somebody, you are making an impact. For many people, actions really do speak louder than words sometimes.

What kinds of acts of service can you perform for others? Basically ask yourself what your partner regularly needs to accomplish or achieve. This could be anything from work-related obligations or planning social occasions to shopping, cleaning, paying bills, walking the dog, doing the laundry, or decorating a party venue. It's literally anything that makes their life easier or takes something off their plate.

Combat your laziness and realize that, to

someone whose love language is acts of service, doing one of these things is like giving them an expensive present. It can be things as simple as household chores, cooking dinner, or going to the post office for them.

None of these are your duty or obligation. In some cases, they might not even be your business or anything you feel any need to be involved in. But that's precisely the point— you are aiming to make *their* lives easier with your service. Try to understand where you can jump in and serve them.

Physical touch. When people touch each other, hormones are released. Physical touch unleashes many biochemical reactions that take people to a different emotional place.

People with this love language also get a level of emotional assurance and comfort through physical contact—anything from hugs, holdings hands, pats on the back, and soft touches on the arm, face, or shoulder. Any type of touch qualifies, really, and has a major impact on a partner who is feeling down or unloved.

A simple hug and kiss can replace gifts and says, "I love you," to people with this love language.

These small points of contact can communicate a wide range of emotions. All of them are positive—love, care, concern, excitement, and arousal. Without physical touch, people may feel as if their partner is being distant and unloving.

It may not even be important to be emotionally present when you use physical touch—to people with this love language, it's a package deal and the emotional connection is implied from physical touch. If you are physically there, it is implied that you are also emotionally and spiritually present.

Physical touch is a natural and necessary part of a relationship, to the extent that if you are sitting with them and not touching them, they may feel something is wrong. Normal for them would be at least holding hands or your hand on their knee. It may be easier to imagine these people as simply needing a certain amount of physical touch when you are near them.

If you're within reaching distance, use touch. Occasionally, go out of your way to sit closer to them so they can touch you—for people with this love language, sometimes just making yourself available and open for their touching is just as important as actively touching them. Kiss them spontaneously a few times a day and this love language will likely be fulfilled.

However, people with this love language are also very attuned to physical movement and touch. This means it can be difficult to engage in small touches if you are just going through the motions—they will see through you. As with the other love languages, physical touch is simply a representation of how much love and affection there is internally.

So where in the spectrum do you fall, and more importantly, where does your partner fall? Mastering the love languages can be one of the most important weapons in your attraction arsenal. You might be as charming as Casanova, but it doesn't matter if you speak a foreign love language. Knowing the appropriate love language allows you to more closely get your intent and emotional message across.

Takeaways:

- There are so many shades of gray in dating, flirting, and attraction. How can you ever be sure that your message is getting across as you want it to? You can never be 100% certain, but learning Gary Chapman's love languages will help you.
- There are five love languages, which are ways of outwardly demonstrating love and affection. You may have more than one, and you probably don't match with your significant other. Therefore, it is important to learn what matters to you and what matters to them so you can reduce misunderstandings and stop feeling taken for granted.

- The five love languages are words of affirmation, physical touch, quality time, acts of service, and gifts. Learn yours and learn your significant other's.

Chapter 7. How to Know What You Want (You Don't)

When I was a teenager, I thought I knew exactly what I wanted in a girlfriend.

[Read this in a teenage perspective]

First, she had to be a ballerina because I had a couple of friends that were ballerinas, and they were pretty, fit, and fun to be around. Maybe it was a side effect of constantly being in spandex and being scrutinized, but they didn't seem to let much rattle them.

Second, they had to have a car because I drove my mother's car and had to split car time with her, which was annoying because she went shopping a lot. The year before, I was almost late to the winter dance because of my mom's dance aerobics class!

Third, they couldn't be painters, because my friend Molly was a painter and the only thing she talked about was the new art she was planning and creating. At first it was nice to hear about something different, but it was getting old pretty fast. I intentionally sat at different table than her at lunch, so I think my message was pretty clear.

[Teenage perspective over]

To many of you, the teenage me sounds simplistic, idealistic, and shallow—call it what you will. That's certainly how I would characterize it.

The teenage me allowed random occurrences and events to shape my views and also cared about things that had no logical connection to anything that would make a good partner. Almost everything had a shallow basis and wasn't about a person's traits or personality. Finally, there were elements that sounded great in theory but were completely unrelated to anything else in my life.

I had essentially created an ideal in my mind without considering whether it made sense for me—or whether it made sense period. That's pretty much par for the course for a teenager who hadn't even had his first kiss yet. You wouldn't expect much more depth from someone who lacks life experience and doesn't have any perspective to base his views on. You might even be impressed that a teenager could articulate three traits or features that way.

Now take that teenager's perspective and imagine it coming out of a grown adult's mouth—at 30 or even 40 old. You'd think that it would be absolutely laughable, but it doesn't sound so unnatural, does it? The truth is, we still fall prey to the same *shiny objects* approach (as in, "Ooh, look at that shiny object! I want that.") that teenagers do when we think about what we want in our partner. We are overly affected by singular experiences and attempt to extrapolate what little information we have into hard requirements or deal-breakers.

Teenage Patrick's first request was for a ballerina because they tend to be fit and pretty. *He was saying that he liked an entire group of people based on an idealized and filtered view of an occupation.*

Teenage Patrick's second request was for someone with a car. *He was saying he wanted people based on their means and resources— like looking at someone's resume or evaluating their income.*

Teenage Patrick's third request was for no painters. *He was saying that he didn't like an entire group of people because his exposure to one person had created a judgment on everyone in that group.*

We still do all of those things as adults! We

say what we *want* based on what we don't really know, and we say what we *don't want* based on what we don't really know—*and* we want someone with means. We still allow the same errors in thinking to guide our decisions in what we want in a mate long after puberty.

We Are Just Guessing

More often than not, we suffer from a lack of information about the things we want and the things we don't want. We have a great time at one party but wonder why we don't enjoy other parties, not realizing that we don't know exactly why we had a good time—and vice versa. It's exactly the same with knowing the type of person you want to be with. Our lives aren't scientific experiments in which we can isolate and prevent confounding factors. We do the best we can with what we have, and we have to make educated assumptions and guesses along the way. We compare our experiences with so-called objective standards, with experiences from our social circle, and we come to a decision.

In the same way, people tend to think they know exactly what they want in a partner. If you ask anyone this question, you'll get a laundry list of traits that seems to come from a place of experience and knowledge. He must be tall, possess a great sense of humor, and love children. She must be adventurous and a willing traveler, drama-free, and great with your mother.

The list of traits never gets much more specific than that, and people end up describing someone who is attractive in an idealistic way or based on incomplete information like Teenage Patrick.

I usually take this to mean that people have no idea what they actually want in a partner. A study in 2008 (Eastwick & Finkel) confirmed this fact when researchers surveyed participants in a speed-dating event. Before the event occurred, the participants completed a questionnaire about the traits they found most attractive in the opposite sex.

The questionnaire found typical results—the participants indicated they were attracted to generic and traditional traits and characteristics. Generally speaking, men placed a higher premium on physical attractiveness, while women placed higher value on status and resources.

After the speed-dating event, people were asked who they were attracted to at the event. And guess what?

There was virtually zero overlap between the traits they *said* they were looking for and the traits they were actually attracted to. People did not act according to how they answered the pre-study questionnaire—to their credit. Men showed interest in a woman's status and personality and weren't generally as shallow as they indicated previously. Women also expanded their range of what they were interested in.

In other words, people were astonishingly bad at predicting what they would be attracted to in other people. You probably didn't need a study to tell you that. The chapter on arranged marriages also provides clarity in how bad we are at predicting what matters in a relationship.

One reason relates to a psychological theory called the *construal-level theory* (Trope & Liberman, 2003). The theory states that psychological *distance* prompts people to think abstractly and ideally about things, while psychological *closeness* prompts people to think more concretely and realistically about things.

For example, if you don't know much about baseball, which represents psychological distance, all you can do is say that there's someone who throws the ball, someone who catches the ball, and someone who hits the ball. That's abstract thinking.

But if you played baseball in school, which represents psychological closeness, you could go on and on about baseball strategy and batting averages. That's concrete thinking.

There are a few factors that influence psychological closeness:

1. Temporal distance—time
2. Spatial distance—proximity
3. Social distance—interpersonal similarity
4. Hypothetical distance—how likely you imagine something to be

When we put the construal-level theory into the dating context, it confirms everything we knew and the prior studies found.

When people met potential romantic partners in person, there was very little psychological distance, which caused them to evaluate the person in front of them in an entirely different way than if they merely thought about the type of romantic partner they wanted—the psychological distance of which would cause them to describe ideal platitudes and traits.

In other words, our daydreams when we're by ourselves are nothing close to how we evaluate people that are right in front of us.

That's one reason people don't know what they want in a partner. We are actually in our heads too much, away from the people we seek to meet, and this causes us to ruminate in psychological distance. The more we plan and make a vision board full of traits we want, the more detached from our actual preferences we are.

Another reason is that people tend to be self-centered and focused on themselves. When we think about our mate preferences, we're often not thinking about attraction and what we actually like. We're thinking about our self-interests and how we would benefit from that type of partner. Everything else flows from that self-interest. Self-interest and benefit can easily become conflated with attraction and even love.

For example, you want a partner with high earning potential because it will bode well for you in the future. You're not thinking about attraction—you're thinking about a long-term view and how your mate will help you reach the vision you have for your own life. It's all very logical and rational—you might even call it cold and calculating.

Of course, logic and rationality rarely mix with the real world of dating and relationships.

Finally, we regularly formulate theories about what we find attractive in others because we think we should feel certain ways and want certain things. It's what we've been socialized with since birth and continue to be socialized with through our parents, families, friends, and the media at large. We are told what to think without considering whether it's the best course of action (type of partner) for us.

If you've been raised since birth to only love pine trees while simultaneously being told that oak trees are bad for you, there's not much chance you'll deviate from pine trees, even if they make you sneeze. Oak trees might be your exact fit, but you'll be fighting years of indoctrination to even be open to them. Even if you're unhappy with pine trees, that doesn't tell you that oak trees will fit you either!

All We know Is No

So what do we actually know about what we want? What do we know that is accurate and not influenced by others, self-interest, or psychological distance? It's starting to feel like everything is just a stab in the dark or a *black box* process that just spits out the ever-elusive *chemistry*.

We do have our own experiences: all we truly learn from our past relationships are specific things we *don't want*—either from a daily interaction perspective (did you want to choke this person when they did this?) or a long-term view (do they want to move to Antarctica while you want to remain somewhere not freezing?).

All our past relationships and experiences teach us is a small set of no's, and that does not mean that we simply want the opposite of what we disliked about a previous partner.

For example, if you dated an extremely

passive person and hated it, all it means is you don't like dating passive people. That's it. It doesn't mean you want and/or need someone who is extremely dominant—that's just an assumption we make about ourselves all the time. All we know is *no*, not that we want the opposite of that.

If you dislike X, Y, and Z, it doesn't mean that you like the opposites of X, Y, and Z (A, B, and C). When you imagine what your partner looks like, they aren't the opposites of traits you dislike. That leads to an overcorrection, where you swing the pendulum too much in the opposite direction and find something that you also hate. For example, if you hated dating an extremely passive person and later tried dating an extremely aggressive person, it doesn't mean that would work out too well.

In the same vein, many people have purported deal-breakers—traits or history they feel they would never accept in a partner.

Most things people think are deal-breakers

for them aren't, actually. The best way to figure out if something is a real deal-breaker is to visualize the following hypothetical: would this tear you apart if you had been dating someone for a year before you discovered the deal-breaker about them? Close that psychological distance and see how it would feel in the moment.

For example, what if your father died from smoking-related cancer and you feel that someone being a smoker is a total deal-breaker. Then, after a year of dating your partner, you discover they occasional smoke a cigarette or two. For this to be a deal-breaker, you would be single again very soon after your discovery. It's probably not a deal-breaker at that point, and thus not a real one. Which means it's just a preference.

On the other hand, what if you discover they don't want children, and you absolutely do? Or that they plan to move to Africa, and you flat out don't want to? Or if their religion is going to force both of you to wear uniforms and move into a cult commune?

Well, those are actual deal-breakers because they are things you truly cannot accept if you feel strongly about them. People have a tendency to characterize too many things as deal-breakers up front, which unnecessarily restricts the number of people they might be open to.

A relationship is a collection of day-to-day moments that fuse together to form a long-term goal, and focusing on deal-breakers and other requirements completely ignores this. We simply have too little information, and once again, *all we know is no*.

Taken as a whole, people don't know what they want in a partner, or they search for the wrong thing because they are *trait-hunting*. People search for traits first, then hope the chemistry and fit are there. Recall that, in the chapter about the business of arranged marriages, this is what they do as well.

Why, then, are there such different results? Because people that do this by themselves are wildly dishonest with themselves about what they are looking for, what traits they can expect, and what they deserve. They want what they want without regard for whether they would be able to get it and whether they would be attractive to someone that possesses those traits.

Is chemistry first, and then looking at the traits, a better approach? The success and stable happiness of arranged marriages might say otherwise.

The only common threads here are that what we want in a partner only becomes clear once we get below the surface and actually spend time with someone. Studies even show that people who are less traditionally attractive become more attractive once people spend time with them and discover their unique appeal (Eastwick, 2014). When you look below the surface, you find things you didn't know you liked, and the things you thought mattered cease to matter so much. It's almost as if there is no substitute for investigating real chemistry.

Universal Desires

And yet (another disclaimer, of course), there are scientifically proven triggers for attraction and arousal. While we might not understand what we are looking for from a personality standpoint, there are universal traits that we want from a psychological and biological standpoint.

Excitement. This springs from one of the most interesting theories of arousal—the *misattribution of arousal* theory.

The misattribution of arousal is the proposition that people aren't necessarily aroused by what's in front of them. Instead, for one reason or another, they enter a state of physical arousal first, and then they attribute the cause of that arousal to what is currently in front of them. They make an assumption that because they are physically aroused in the presence of their partner, for example, that their partner was the one arousing them.

Why is this called the *misattribution* of arousal theory? It's because we aren't always correct about what turns us on and gets us physically aroused. This is something you can take advantage of.

In 1974, Donald Dutton and Arthur Aron tested this theory by having two groups of men interact with an attractive female immediately after crossing a bridge. In one group, the bridge was relatively unstable and scary, and the other group's bridge was stable and secure. The attractive female gave her phone number to each and every participant. What ended up happening?

The men in the first group, the scary bridge group, were twice as likely to call the attractive female and ask her on a date after the study was over.

What accounted for this massive difference? Males in the scary bridge group were already aroused when they met and spoke with the attractive female. As a result, they contacted the female because they misattributed their arousal to the female, not the scary bridge they had just crossed. In other words, they believed they were feeling sexual arousal from the female instead of plain old physiological arousal from the fear of the bridge.

The more physically anxious, excited, and even fearful you are, no matter the cause, the more attractive and arousing you will find the people near you because of the misattribution of arousal theory. Here, the scary bridge physically aroused the men in that group and pumped up their adrenaline and bodily functions in a way similar to when we are sexually aroused.

This certainly happens more than you might think. People misattribute physiological arousal to sexual attraction all the time. Many even do it by instinct.

For example, have you ever taken a date, or been taken, on a roller coaster, flying, or something else that's thrilling over a dinner date? Even a scary movie qualifies here. If you have, or if you've heard this advice parroted around, it's because it takes advantage of the misattribution of arousal theory. Your date gets physiologically aroused and excited by the roller coaster or scary movie, grabs your hand out of fear, and then attributes the butterflies in his or her stomach to you and not the triple-faced ghost on the movie screen.

It's also what dating reality shows like *The Bachelor* and *The Bachelorette* use in spades. They'll send their contestants out on thrilling and dangerous dates like skydiving or deep ocean shark fighting. How can you expect sparks not to fly after that due to this theory? Creating excitement is a no-brainer if you want to instantly create attraction.

Gender-specific triggers. Though arousal is universal in some ways, it can also be incredibly nuanced. There is a very marked gender difference in the basics of arousal— the hows and whys, even.

Researcher and author Emily Nagoski discovered through various studies that men are spontaneously aroused, while women become aroused in response to something.

It means that men spontaneously have the desire to have sex, and women have that same desire only in response to that man. This is the cause of what many couples consider mismatched libidos—the man will be the only one to initiate sex, while the woman may be happy to have it but will never outwardly show signs of desire and lust.

This commonly causes men to feel unwanted and neglected, but it's a matter of adjusting expectations because women don't function in the same spontaneous manner. In fact, Nagoski estimated that up to one-third of women have primarily responsive sexual arousal, whereas the vast majority of men have primarily spontaneous sexual arousal.

How can we bridge the gap here? It's the knowledge that women need to be aroused first before they want to have sex, while men continually just want sex. Their desire may not actually be different; you just have to set the conditions for one gender a little bit more.

The lesson for men is that you have to seduce women first, and then they will be open to sex. Women are looking for cues from you to be aroused because it won't happen for them out of thin air. The lesson for women is to not feel guilty or shame if you have been told you have a low sex drive or libido. You just may have responsive sexual arousal, and your partner needs to break the ice a little bit more first—or you can break it yourself first, but don't have the expectation that you should spontaneously feel horny or aroused while shopping for apples.

Recent studies published in the sexology journal of *Archives of Sexual Behavior* confirm the assertion that women need to be outwardly desired more than men before they feel aroused themselves.

The studies found that a major part of female

sexual arousal and fantasies was perceiving themselves to be desirable, irresistible, and like men couldn't control themselves around them. If a woman perceives herself to be the object of desire, lust, and affection, then her sexual arousal and appetite are generally higher than if not.

That certainly adds fuel to the fire that women are more responsive and dependent on signals from their partner in order to feel attractive and sexually aroused. I hope the men reading are paying attention here. Women won't typically be the ones to spontaneously come up behind you and start copping a feel, but they won't mind if you do (if you have previous signs of consent and attraction).

And if you do it consistently and in a way that makes them feel like you can't help or control yourself around them, you'll be able to have sex more consistently because you are catering to their responsive sense of sexual arousal.

Laughter. A sense of humor is highly attractive to the opposite sex. However, again, there was a big difference between how genders perceived this seemingly simple statement. The female definition of a good sense of humor was when the male made them laugh, but the male definition of a good sense of humor was when the female laughed at their jokes. Another researcher analyzed over 3000 dating profiles, and the data lined up with the previous findings: women tended to describe their ability to appreciate humor, whereas men tended to describe their ability to produce humor.

It also lines up with traditional gender roles of the suitor and the recipient, so perhaps no matter how close we get to true gender equality, there are still hardwired preferences when it comes to romantic and sexual relations.

Voice. Dr. Susan Hughes of Albright College discovered that these hardwired preferences that prefer biological differences are highly present in the voices of the opposite sex.

Women were found to be more attracted to men who spoke in lower, baritone or bass voices, and men were found to be far more attracted to women who spoke in higher, soprano pitches. If you want a reference for how that sounds, just think Marilyn Monroe singing *Happy Birthday* to John F. Kennedy or any of Barry White's songs and you have the general idea.

What we've learned about desirable traits is that even though we are consistently wrong about what we want, at least there are biological bases we can rely on. At least it makes us a little more predictable in our lack of accuracy.

Takeaways:

- We often think we know what we want based on singular experiences, stereotypes, or simple social pressures. But we are typically very, very wrong.
- In fact, most of the time, we are just making educated guesses. Psychological distance is deceptive, and we often

confuse what we want with what benefits us from a self-interest standpoint. In reality, what we do know is simply what we don't want. This is not the same as wanting the opposite of what we don't want.

- Despite our own internal confusions, there are certain scientifically proven traits we do seek in mates that are more related to biological imperatives. We are subconsciously drawn to excitement and arousal, fulfilling gender-specific arousal triggers, a sense of humor, and masculine and feminine voices.

Chapter 8. Acts of the Amorous Nature

Much of this book has been focused on how to get to this point: intimate relations.

When you have successfully engineered attraction to the point where you can consummate that attraction, congratulations! You've reached the peak and there is nothing left to think about. You've won and everything is downhill from here.

That would be nice if that were the truth. It seems like the end goal might be to have sex with someone, but in reality, the goal is to have sustained, intimate sex with someone.

That is a very different goal because of how much it encompasses and the hoops to jump through for it.

In essence, we're talking about how to achieve remarkable sex. Some people might view sex like pizza; even bad pizza is still a good meal. But if we want to fulfill our real goals of sex that accentuates an emotional bond and that can lead to a relationship, we can't just take our cues from pornography. Sex is one of the most primal drives—as such, as with before, this can make us relatively predictable in a way that you can take advantage of.

Here's the thing about great, toe-curling sex: it isn't what we think it is. We have continually been told one spicy, "secret" sex position or delving into blindfolds and whips and chains just because it's novel and exciting. At least, that's what magazine covers have sold us.

Much of what we think makes for great sex is split into one of two camps. It's either about specific techniques you can be doing better or more of, or it's about spicing up your sex life in ways that simply blow your mind because they tap into your deeper and darker fetishes.

While those are true and undoubtedly help, they are also misleading. They can sometimes cause us to skip over the basics and what really matters, like buying a car with a terrible engine but a nice paint job and door handles. You might think you're going to have a smooth ride, and you might for the first couple of times, but it's not destined for success and can undermine your other efforts at creating remarkable sex from the inside and out.

If wonderful sex isn't about novelty, Isn't about exciting fetishes, and isn't about the specific techniques and positions, what is it about? Well, this might be a relief for you if you feel that sex just doesn't need to involve superhuman fitness or leather props.

Researcher Peggy Kleinplatz conducted multiple studies on the issue and found one particular set of elements that were far more indicative to great sex than novelty or spiciness. In fact, those elements that you'll always read about on the covers of magazines did not figure into the results. They didn't report helping people's sex lives at all! In the end, it was advice that sounded good in theory but didn't make a difference in practice.

No toys or tongue tricks are needed to create remarkable sex. Kleinplatz also found in the study that actual orgasms and attraction were not part of what made remarkable sex. This is good news for some and terrible news for others. It almost sounds like I am about to sell you the one special technique that blows all others out of the water, but it's really about bringing it back to the basics.

She found eight elements that thousands of respondents in her studies listed as the most important, and these elements were consistent across all age groups, genders, ethnicities, and even locations. The eight elements of great sex are listed below, and we'll go through each in greater detail.

The elements are:

1. Presence
2. Connection
3. Intimacy
4. Communication
5. Authenticity
6. Bliss
7. Exploration
8. Vulnerability

As you might figure, some of these elements are fulfilled by what magazines tell us to do—with novelty, whips, and chains. However, you might miss the point if you don't think about the actual purpose and intention behind the elements.

Presence. What does presence mean? It's not a magnetic presence at a party; rather, it's the act of being *present* and in the moment. This is when you're not preoccupied, and you're completely focused on the person in front of you and the act that is occurring. You have only one thing in your mind, and that is the other person and how they feel.

You act like the other person is your world for the moment—and they are, aren't they? You have to commit all the way with your time and attention and fully immerse yourself in the moment.

You can't be a spectator, judge, critic, or passive participant. You're not thinking about your emails, your television shows, or what you want to have for dinner. If you're on this wavelength, then it's no wonder your sex life is on thin ice.

You are simply there, fully present, with nothing else on your mind. The world comprises only two individuals, one bed, and passion. Everything else is put on the back burner and essentially disappears. That's what it means to be present.

It's easy to see how we can fall prey to not being present. We all have numerous responsibilities throughout the day. But various studies peg the average length of sexual intercourse at anywhere from seven to sixteen minutes. It should not be a tremendous struggle to shut down your brain for that amount of time and simply lose yourself. Just imagine how present you would be having sex in a cabin in the woods, with no television or Internet access. That's the kind of focus and connection you want every time.

They deserve it, and so do you. How would you feel if someone prefaced sex with, "Let's be quick. I have more work," or if they continually looked at a clock during the act? Being present during sex, you will be more attentive, respond better to people's signs, and care more about their satisfaction.

Connection. This is when you feel like you're in sync with the other person mentally and emotionally. You understand things without having to say them, you know each other, and you feel an emotional pull toward them. You have electric chemistry and both of you know it.

Contrast that to a one-night stand, where you probably have very little emotional investment. The act and ensuing pleasure is minimized because there's little at stake and it's purely physical. With emotional connection, you create something with intimacy, and you are fusing your bodies and minds together for a brief moment in time.

Connection is feeling a spark with the other person holistically, not just physically. You like them on more than just a physical level, and you can experience feeling bonded with them. When you have a strong connection, you might say things like, "Our bodies just moved together and we didn't have to say a word."

Intimacy. This can be distinguished from connection because intimacy is about a deeper caring and love for the other person, whereas connection might be momentary and fleeting. When you have that type of feeling toward someone, then sex becomes more than just a physical act. It becomes an act of love and sharing.

This is also a complete acceptance of the other person and their flaws, and it involves you opening yourself to them. This happens when you respect and care for someone, and it is a byproduct of a healthy relationship. There is trust, vulnerability, and the feeling that you can bare yourself to someone else.

Communication. Communication is key in friendships and relationships, so it should be in sex as well. From another angle, sex is an activity with a partner (or multiple partners), so it only makes sense that there should be a healthy amount of communication to coordinate, discuss, direct, and request whenever appropriate. Greater satisfaction simply occurs when collaboration is possible, and collaboration is possible with better communication.

Along with communication comes a heightened attention and empathy to your partner's needs and desires. This is important because sex should not be approached like a self-centered act—it's an act with one goal:

an orgasm for both parties. In fact, the best sex focuses on the other person's pleasure, so communicating what those might be is paramount.

Communication should be open, there should be mutual support, and there should be an ability for both parties to express exactly what they want or dislike without the fear of judgment or rejection. This is where talking about fetishes and kinks comes in, because open and honest communication should allow those without feeling self-conscious or judged.

You should ideally be able to communicate about everything, from exactly what you hate to the tiny things you love. The point is to keep a running dialogue going because preferences can always change, and you need to be able to adapt to them.

Authenticity. Remarkable sex is honest and open. It's authentic because you aren't hiding anything. Not only are you making yourself completely open to the other person, but you're trusting your body with them. If you can let go and make yourself vulnerable, it can be powerful.

You are being authentic and honest about what you like and dislike, and you are encouraging the same in the other person. You are having sex for pleasure, love, or expression, not for any nefarious reason or ulterior motives. Put another way, you feel that you can be genuine in your expression, that you aren't hiding or inhibiting your desires, and that you can be completely transparent and honest with the other person.

You should feel free to do, touch, lick, and suck what you like without embarrassment or feelings of judgment. This works both ways, because both parties need to ensure that they don't make the other feel judged or guilty. Truly authentic sex is liberating because you feel like you can do what you like without having to restrain yourself. Of course, that works best with communication and the other elements in this chapter.

Bliss. This is a loaded word. What does it mean here?

It means that amazing sex is more than just an act. It's a mental state of mind, and it creates something that is more than the sum of its parts. It creates an emotion of transcendence and bliss: a peaceful state of mind characterized by happiness, transformation, introspection, and fulfillment.

It's a state of nirvana. You're in a world that consists of only two people, and you feel like there's nowhere else you'd rather be at that moment. You are exchanging mental, emotional, and physical energy. You are basking in their glow and pleasure.

Bliss just means you feel fulfilled and satisfied after the act, with no regret. Your head is clear, you feel more at peace with the world, and you have gained perspective on life. Some people might have sex to calm their nerves, out of boredom, out of hatred, or out of pure lust. Blissfully remarkable sex is when sex occurs as an expression of love and fulfillment with the other person.

You can even think about bliss in religious terms. You feel a sense of peace that you may receive after praying or a particularly powerful religious service. That's what sex can do at times. It can feel like a holy experience.

Exploration. This, of course, is also where kink and spicy sex come into play.

Sex can sometimes get boring, even with all of the other elements in this chapter, so exploration, or at least being willing to explore and indulge, is a key to remarkable sex.

It's fun. It breaks you out of your routine, and it makes sex novel and interesting, which is necessary sometimes. It allows you to discover what you really want and to test uncharted waters. When you can explore your sexuality, you can also discover what makes you orgasm the longest and hardest. It might not be what you think, and you never would have discovered it if you didn't open your mind.

Exploration can sometimes mean a certain amount of risk, but risk in this context isn't really risk. It's just stepping outside of your comfort zone, and there aren't any negative consequences other than to say, "Well, I didn't like that as much as I thought I would. Next!" The only risk here is that you might buy something expensive to explore a fetish and end up hating it and feel that you wasted that money.

Exploration puts the fun back into sex. It makes it an unpredictable ride that is the essence of playing. You can follow your instincts and discover new kinks you like, or you can just allow curiosity to guide you. You can play sex games to have fun during long car rides, or you can try to make the other person orgasm as many times as possible within 24 hours.

These are all possible with exploration and stepping outside of your comfort zone. Remarkable sex is comfortable with laughter, getting messy, and new acts for their own sake. It doesn't restrain or judge them—it encourages them.

Vulnerability. Scary. We all know what happens when we make ourselves vulnerable. It allows us to be hurt.

However, remarkable sex requires this because of the positives and benefits it can allow. It allows us to fully embrace someone and let them into our hearts and psyches and bodies. We are physically naked during sex, but vulnerability allows us to drop our mental and emotional shields. You are trusting someone and surrendering to them. This is scary.

You are shedding your defense mechanisms, your anxieties, and your egos to the sexual encounter. You are stripping bare, putting yourself on a shelf for judgment, and trusting that the other person will celebrate you rather than reject you. You are devoted to them and trust that they are devoted to you. You say and do things that you would never do to other people, but here you aren't embarrassed because it's what is in your heart.

In fact, you say exactly what you want to say and do that as well. That's vulnerability— when you don't filter and you allow people inside your walls. Fantastic and remarkable sex is pulling others closer to you when you feel the exact opposite impulse and you want to keep someone at arm's length.

Again, you can see that none of these elements of remarkable sex are what we usually think they are: novelty and techniques. Those are included and a part of some of these elements, but not the underlying aspect that makes it so satisfying and pleasurable.

Kleinplatz's findings are important because they tell us that wonderful sex does not depend on flexibility, athleticism, or being choked so hard that you nearly fall unconscious. Wonderful sex is for everyone because it happens when you simply focus on the other person, give yourself freely, and have an authentic connection.

While that may be harder to find than a one-night stand, it also means that everyone in a relationship can indeed have remarkable sex. Nothing keeps you from it except yourself. If you find yourself unable to satisfy any of the elements, the problem is never in the sex itself. Nearly everyone has the mental and physical capability to fulfill Kleinplatz's factors for great sex. It may not be easy, however, and thus it comes down to how much you care and want the sex to improve. You have the blueprint; what you do with It is up to you.

It's never a bad thing to do a bit more exploring, however.

Getting Kinky

Fifty Shades of Grey. There, I mentioned it.

The infamous book was important for introducing the concept of kinky and abnormal sexual practices into the collective conscious of the general population. It shone a flashlight into the dark depths of the kink world and gave it a name—Christian Grey.

It gave people an outlet to explore and provided some kind of framework into things they vaguely enjoyed but had no way of articulating.

Kinky sex has always been a point of captivation for people because it involves sex, a topic usually greeted with blushes, giggles, and knowing glances. Fascination ensues when people realize they could be having much more fulfilling sex than they are currently having.

Kink arrived loudly and is here to stay, but it is not without its critics. The critics are largely a factor of judgments and a misunderstanding of the simple fact that people have different tastes.

It's such a simple analogy that I've used it time and time again; some people love football and some people love baseball. If you ask them to articulate the reason for their preference, most people will say, "I don't know, just because I do." Now substitute any number of fetishes for football and vanilla sex with baseball. What's the real difference here? Would you prevent someone from watching football just as you would purport to prevent empowering someone to seize their own pleasure?

But the science of kink and how it relates to attraction is fascinating and indicates that it might go deeper than a simple preference for football or leather whips.

It turns out that some of us might actually be biologically predisposed to some sexual kinks and couldn't help it if we tried. Neural mapping, the literal physical configuration of our brains, might explain our proclivity for some sexual kinks. If not the brain structure, then the neurotransmitters might explain it.

At least, those are two of the theories I will explore shortly.

What is the science of kink and the cause behind some of our deepest and darkest desires? There are five distinct theories that have been set forth that attempt to explain why we like what we do (Justin Lehmiller, Harvard University).

Adjacent brain theory. This is a theory put forth by Dr. V.S. Ramachandran of the University of California, San Diego, and utilizes an understanding of the brain's physical structure to explain kinky interests.

Different parts of the brain govern different body parts and bodily functions. This has been proven extensively, to the point where we now understand exactly where in the brain speech, personality, and anger occur. There are also specific parts of the brain that govern sexual impulses.

Now, it's not as if there are walls in the brain to keep these parts from interacting, talking, and physically overlapping with each other. The adjacent brain theory states that adjacent regions of the brain do in fact show associated activity, which means that the brain region that controls sexual impulse may very well be adjacent to the brain region that controls anger or specific body parts.

For example, the adjacent brain theory easily explains the common foot fetish because the brain regions responsible for sexual impulses, the genitalia, and the feet are close to each other and interact. When there is brain activity in one region, there is some brain activity in all adjacent regions.

The adjacent brain theory explains many aspects of kink, specifically ones that involve sexual infatuations with nonsexual body parts. But that is only a sliver of the range of kinks that exist, and the following theories can address most of them.

Pavlovian conditioning theory. Even if you don't have any interest in psychology, you are probably familiar with Ivan Pavlov and his dog.

Pavlov conducted experiments on his dog to test the subconscious routines that are created in response to predictable stimuli. He began serving dinner to his dog and accompanied dinner with ringing a bell. The dog salivated in anticipation of the food. Soon, Pavlov removed the dinner entirely and only rang the bell. The dog still salivated as if the food were present.

It showed that when people were conditioned to respond to two stimuli, the same response will come with only one stimuli present.

In the 1960s, a group of men were shown images of naked women interspersed with images of boots. As predictable by conditioning, the men were conditioned to respond with sexual arousal to the two stimuli, and when they were shown only pictures of the boots, they still responded by being sexually aroused.

This study proved that it's possible to form

sexual associations with just about anything if the requisite amount of conditioning (voluntary or not) has occurred.

If you have sex or are aroused in the presence of a green teddy bear, all subsequent teddy bears or green furry objects might be enough to trigger your libido. Some might call that a kink, while some might call that a normal Saturday night. The key to this theory is that there is repeated exposure during periods of sexual arousal—it can even be certain smells, locations, or articles of clothing.

Gross-out theory. The gross-out theory was put forth by Lehmiller, and it essentially states that when people are sexually aroused, they care much less about anything else, including things that would detract from their sense of arousal. Notably, their *disgust impulse* is reduced.

In other words, when you are highly sexually aroused, you just want to get off or have an orgasm, and nothing besides pending bodily harm will throw you off that goal. Sounds about right to me. Sometimes you might inadvertently play with or stumble into things that would normally disgust you, such as feces, bodily fluids, or anal play. But then you realize that you didn't mind it, or even liked it, so you continue to integrate it into your sex life.

I recall a story from a friend I won't name who had recently broken his leg that epitomizes exactly how the gross-out theory works in real life. He was also newly single and had a hot date that he had to struggle to get to in his crutches. The date went well, and matters got hot and heavy back at her apartment later that night. I received a call at 7:00 a.m. the next morning from my friend begging me to come pick him up because he thought he had broken his leg again during vigorous sex.

Clearly, the gross-out theory applies in a wider sense as well.

Pain theory. *It hurts so good.*

Decades of research in neuroscience have shown that neurotransmitters, the chemicals in our brain that help us process our external world, are used for multiple purposes. There are only so many neurotransmitters, and they are released in certain combinations and batches to influence how good or bad we feel.

It just so happens that most of the neurotransmitters involved in sexual pleasure and pain are the same, such as serotonin, dopamine, and adrenaline.

It's as if the external signals are processed and sent to the brain on the same highway. So if pain and sexual pleasure both independently release similar combinations of neurotransmitters in our brains, then it makes too much sense to just combine the two.

This would explain the origin of many aspects of kink, such as physical dominance, whips, chains, choking, spanking, and even autoerotic asphyxiation. People don't realize they are doing it not just for the direct physical pleasure, but also the release of sweet dopamine and serotonin in their brains.

One might suppose that the ever-popular rape fantasy also slots into this category. Rape play similarly releases adrenaline, dopamine, and serotonin. This means that the pain in the *pain theory* doesn't have to be actual physical pain. As long as there is the element of threat and anticipation of pain, it's enough of a threat for the proper neurotransmitters to be released and work toward sexual arousal.

The pain theory and the gross-out theory explain many of the kinks that are beyond the realm of many people's understanding.

Subjective normal theory. The last theory to explain the appeal of kink and kinky sex derives from a study conducted by Meredith Chivers in 2014.

She gathered an all-female group of subjects and split them based on whether they were interested in BSDM (whips, chains, leather, and such) or not. Both groups watched two types of pornography: kinky and vanilla.

The women that were interested in BSDM had the same rate of vaginal blood flow as the non-kinky women who watched vanilla pornography. Likewise, when the kinky women watched vanilla porn, their blood flow did not increase at all. This was a predictable result in some ways. People were aroused by what they indicated their preference was, but people were not aroused by what they were not interested in.

People just have different desires and concepts of what an arousing sexual encounter looks like, and they aren't interested in other people's concepts. This study suggests that there is nothing neurologically abnormal about people that have kinkier sexual desires than others.

Some people enjoy sour foods and some people love salty foods. In theory, we are biologically the same, but we all have slight variations, and these variations don't mean our tongues are defective. Everyone has their subjective version of what's normal and vanilla, even though it might be shocking and extreme to someone else.

So the fifth and final theory of what causes kink? It completely reframes what kink is—it's just a preference, not an indication of anything suspicious or unbalanced. Nothing out of the ordinary had to occur for it to arise.

Naturally, you might assume that having the same tastes in sexual kinks would ensure sexual compatibility or at least overcome a huge hurdle to that, being that sexual incompatibility lists as a major and prevalent reason for broken relationships.

A recent study (de Jong & Reiss, 2014) proved that sexual compatibility isn't necessarily about liking the same kinks, though that obviously helps considerably. The study surveyed what kind of sexual activities each member of a couple liked, as well as how much they thought their partner enjoyed those activities. In other words, this survey would be able to determine how similar a couple's sexual preferences were and how complementary they were. Finally, they were surveyed about the amount of satisfaction they had with their sex life.

Surprisingly, similarity and sharing the same kinks was *not* the largest predictor of sexual satisfaction in a couple.

Instead, the only consistent predictor was how *complementary* the sexual preferences were for a couple. In other words, there is more sexual satisfaction to be had if one person likes being tied up and the other enjoys doing the tying—complementary—than if both people enjoy being tied up—similarity.

It seems obvious when you lay it out as such, but it's not so clear in practice. People categorize kink into large, general areas that don't accurately portray what someone actually enjoys sexually.

For example, if you show a sexual interest in feet, you might just want to worship someone else's feet but never have anyone touch yours. There is a distinct difference between the two. Sexual compatibility is about having complementary kinks, not similar ones, which means that you should seek out a partner who can give you what you want and vice versa, not necessarily a partner who wants exactly what you want.

Sometimes the two might overlap, and those are the most fortunate of circumstances.

Kink at some point should probably be downgraded into a mere sexual preference instead of evidence of a traumatic childhood. The science supports this in the way that some people like cilantro, while others can't stand it. Neither are defective, and both deserve to live their lives the way they want.

Engineer attraction and feelings of love through understanding how kinks work, and seek to complement others in bed to keep them coming back for more. What keeps us from exploring them more freely?

Perhaps you saw some porn that seemed really up your alley in all sorts of surprising ways. But none of that matters if you can't bring it up with your partner and have it done to you! Why are we afraid of approaching our partners, and why are we shy in a way that we normally wouldn't be?

Because we are afraid of them judging us. Rather than attempt to convince you away from this fear, I'll just say this: they've seen you naked and know what your orgasm face looks like. They've already judged you and are still having sex with you. They know that people like different things and that vanilla missionary sex isn't ideal for everyone.

If you're with a good partner, you won't be judged for wanting to try something new. They should actually encourage openness, expressiveness, and hearing your true feelings and preferences. And that should run both ways. Remind them that you aren't there to judge them and you might even want to reveal something vulnerable about yourself to set the open and nonjudgmental tone.

You can bring up the topic of kinks in two ways. The first is the direct way, and you already know it and want to avoid it. Therefore, the second method is a bit more incidental and spontaneous in nature. There is a big difference between "Hey, sit down. We need to talk about something" versus a casual "Hey, I just heard about this. What do you think?"

If you want to be slightly more indirect and feel safer doing this, you can concoct a story about the kink or spice that you want to introduce into your sex life.

"I just read about this kink... what do you think?" or "My friend just told me he did this... what do you think?"

That way, you aren't making a direct suggestion; you are simply bringing the topic up and gauging a reaction. When introducing your ideas, however you do it, the key is to not be aggressive or 100% excited and forward about it. This might make them feel obligated to do it, even if they know they would hate it, if they see how strongly you want something. Don't push too hard, because then it will cause one party to be happy and the other party be to silent and resentful.

That's another reason why bringing it up spontaneously and not as a sit-down topic is better. Just put it out there and see how they feel about it without any pressure or expectation from you. The last thing you want your partner to feel is pressure or expectation. Create a safe space for them to talk about what they want and also turn down what they don't want.

If you're feeling bold, you can visit a sex shop for the same purpose. You are in the business of gauging reactions.

If all else fails, investigate using a website such as mojoupgrade.com, which lets you fill out kinks separately and only notifies you on what you match on. More importantly, it does not list the fetishes and kinks that only one person has listed. Therefore, it is a completely safe way to say what you want because they won't see what you've marked if they haven't also marked it.

After all, what good is exploration if you can't proverbially whip it out?

Takeaways:

- At this point in the book, you may have a better understanding of how to reach your goal of mating. However, in reality, your goal is sustained mating within a relationship. How can you make sure the sex is good enough to do that?
- Many sex tips focus on either specific techniques or exploring kinks to improve your sex life, but that's not what really matters. Studies have shown eight specific elements of great sex: presence, connection, intimacy, communication, authenticity, bliss, exploration, and vulnerability. This is empowering because

it means literally everyone has the ability to be a great lover; it just takes time, energy, and attention.

- Exploring kinks, however, is never a bad thing. To do so, it's important to understand how a kink you come across, including yours, may have arisen. There are typically five theories on the matter: adjacent brain theory, Pavlovian conditioning, pain, gross-out theory, and subjective normal theory.

- Yet, knowing your kinks and how they formed is of no use if you don't feel comfortable enough in bringing them up. You may find it easier to bring it up as a side topic purely to gauge reactions and create a safe space to talk about them.

Conclusion

Michael, the client from the introduction, is still a client to this day. Even though he's had what most would consider wonderful successes with women in the past couple of years, he still asks me for my opinion on a wide range of issues.

I realize that, in most cases, he's actually asking for my intuition on humans and how they interact with each other. For most of his questions, that might be sufficient. I can absolutely help with building rapport, text messaging, and date-planning—these are all things that I have had a plethora of experience with myself, so my firsthand experience can guide me.

But some of his questions can benefit greatly from a scientific basis in addition with my firsthand experiences. I did my research so that you don't have to. Having a bit of hard evidence makes advising that one friend that will never listen to you more palatable, no?

Attraction and feelings of love aren't easily engineered, but knowing our biological and psychological blueprint helps.

Sincerely,

Patrick King
Social Interaction Specialist and Conversation Coach
www.PatrickKingConsulting.com

P.S. If you enjoyed this book, please don't be shy and drop me a line, leave a review, or both! I love reading feedback, and reviews are the lifeblood of Kindle books, so they are always welcome and greatly appreciated.

Cheat Sheet

Chapter 1. Animal Attraction

- The classic sociobiological theory of attraction states that we are nothing but animals when it comes to attraction. Worse yet, most of what we are attracted to is subconscious and not fully understood.
- Waisman's four steps are an elaboration on the classic sociobiological theory of attraction. They inform us as to exactly what we are looking for in a way that fuses sociobiological theory with modern dating.
- The four attractions are physical, status, emotion, and logic. It is a sequence you must pass through for a deep and fulfilling relationship, although we know many that only satisfied two or three factors in their own relationships.
- The best way to use these four factors is to understand what phase you are in when you are evaluating someone and to understand where you may fall short.

Chapter 2. Don't Say a Word

- Many animals don't have verbal languages. This means they must communicate their attraction, often forcefully, through their movements and actions. The human equivalent is how we communicate nonverbally with our body language, eye contact, and touching.

- There are different types of attractive body language for each gender. They do, however, depend on the factors of availability and fertility. Simply put, the more available you appear, the more attractive you will be, and the more fertile (this varies by gender) you appear, the more attractive you will be.

- We all know eye contact is import, but it goes beyond simple trustworthiness and confidence. If you are able to use the "sticky eyes" technique, you will begin to create the discomfort and excitement of sexual tension.

- There have been found to be three types of touching in the context of flirting and attraction: friendly, plausible deniability, and nuclear. The most ideal mix is plausible deniability touching mixed with nuclear touching because of the message it sends and how it balances itself out. Friendly touching doesn't really factor into it, even though that's what we are most accustomed to.

Chapter 3. The "Chase"

- The chase is something we subconsciously do, despite outwardly decrying having to play dating games.
- Mostly, the chase has to do with the appeal and addictiveness of intermittent rewards and understanding why human nature works this way.
- The other portion of the chase is about how unavailability is attractive because we immediately begin to ruminate on what we are missing out on and what we are being deprived of.
- However, the chase is not a foolproof method, even though it takes advantage of human psychology. Most of us have been faced with being rejected and told that we are only thought of as friends and

not romantic partners. Is there a way to deal with this?

- For females, perhaps. Studies have shown that females do indeed see males platonically, but males do not do the same for females. Can males and females be only platonic friends? Yes, but it will usually be the female's choice.

Chapter 4. All About Flirting

- Flirting is hard to define, but in general, the goal is to gain someone's attention and make it known that you are interested in them. There are many ways to do this, but not everything will work for everyone.

- Hence, researchers have articulated five distinct flirting styles: physical, polite, traditional, playful, and sincere. It's important to ask what you can use best and what your paramour will best respond to. Having more tools in your tool bag is always a good thing.

- Researchers have additionally discovered a three-step process people who were successful in leaving with someone from bars used consistently. The three steps are approach, synchronize, and touch. It's important to analyze what you are doing, what you are not doing, and if you are skipping over a step or staying on one too long. You should also consider how your flirting style fits into this process.

Chapter 5. Love Is All That Matters…

- Love is what most of us marry for, but arranged marriages have been around for a very long time. In fact, what most of us would consider romantic love is a luxury that is only a few hundred years old.
- Arranged marriages work precisely because love is placed as a low priority. Instead, commitment, problem-solving, and lowered expectations take the forefront and create conditions that allow for a harmonious relationship to first blossom, which allows love to follow.
- Another factor that appears to be more important than love in relationships is similarity. Studies have shown that similarity is more important because people don't tend to change, and over time, you're just left with conflicting

values and worldviews.
- A study specified the traits that predicted the most relationship success if similar: agreeableness and emotional stability.

Chapter 6. Diagnose Yourself

- There are so many shades of gray in dating, flirting, and attraction. How can you ever be sure that your message is getting across as you want it to? You can never be 100% certain, but learning Gary Chapman's love languages will help you.
- There are five love languages, which are ways of outwardly demonstrating love and affection. You may have more than one, and you probably don't match with your significant other. Therefore, it is important to learn what matters to you and what matters to them so you can reduce misunderstandings and stop feeling taken for granted.
- The five love languages are words of affirmation, physical touch, quality time, acts of service, and gifts. Learn yours and learn your significant other's.

Chapter 7. How to Know What You Want (You Don't)

- We often think we know what we want based on singular experiences, stereotypes, or simple social pressures. But we are typically very, very wrong.
- In fact, most of the time, we are just making educated guesses. Psychological distance is deceptive, and we often confuse what we want with what benefits us from a self-interest standpoint. In reality, what we do know is simply what we don't want. This is not the same as wanting the opposite of what we don't want.
- Despite our own internal confusions, there are certain scientifically proven traits we do seek in mates that are more related to biological imperatives. We are subconsciously drawn to excitement and arousal, fulfilling gender-specific arousal triggers, a sense of humor, and masculine and feminine voices.

Chapter 8. Acts of the Amorous Nature

- At this point in the book, you may have a better understanding of how to reach your goal of mating. However, in reality, your goal is sustained mating within a relationship. How can you make sure the sex is good enough to do that?
- Many sex tips focus on either specific techniques or exploring kinks to improve your sex life, but that's not what really matters. Studies have shown eight specific elements of great sex: presence, connection, intimacy, communication, authenticity, bliss, exploration, and vulnerability. This is empowering because it means literally everyone has the ability to be a great lover; it just takes time, energy, and attention.
- Exploring kinks, however, is never a bad thing. To do so, it's important to understand how a kink you come across, including yours, may have arisen. There are typically five theories on the matter: adjacent brain theory, Pavlovian conditioning, pain, gross-out theory, and subjective normal theory.

- Yet, knowing your kinks and how they formed is of no use if you don't feel comfortable enough in bringing them up. You may find it easier to bring it up as a side topic purely to gauge reactions and create a safe space to talk about them.

www.ingramcontent.com/pod-product-compliance
Lightning Source LLC
Chambersburg PA
CBHW070922030426
42336CB00014BA/2500